The Gold Archive #5

SPOCK'S BRAIN

By Nick Joy

THE GOLD ARCHIVE

SPOCK'S BRAIN

ISBN: 9781913456252

Published by Obverse Books, Edinburgh

Range Editors: Paul Simpson and Stuart Douglas

Cover Design: Cody Schell

First edition: February 2022

10 9 8 7 6 5 4 3 2 1

Text © 2021 Nick Joy

No part of this publication may be reproduced, stored in a retrieval system, or transmitted, in any form or by any means without the prior written permission of the publisher, nor be otherwise circulated in any form of binding or cover other than that in which it is published and without a similar condition being imposed on the subsequent purchaser.

A CIP catalogue record for this title is available from the British Library.

CONTENTS

Chapter 1: Teaser

Chapter 2: Number One And Yeoman

Chapter 3: The Theiss Titillation Theory

Chapter 5: Version Control

Chapter 6: 'If Only'

Chapter 7: Future Imperfect

Appendix: Adaptations

Bibliography

Acknowledgements

Biography

OVERVIEW

Episode Title: *Spock's Brain*

Writer: Lee Cronin (aka Gene L Coon)

Director: Marc Daniels

Original US Transmission Date: 20 September 1968

First UK airdate: 13 October 1971

Stardate: 5431.4

Running Time: 50m

Regular Cast: William Shatner (Kirk), Leonard Nimoy (Spock), DeForest Kelley (McCoy), George Takei (Sulu), James Doohan (Scott), Nichelle Nichols (Uhura), Walter Koenig (Chekov), Majel Barrett (Nurse Chapel)

Guest Cast: James Daris (Creature), Marj Dusay (Kara), Sheila Leighton (Luma)

Uncredited Cast: William Blackburn (Hadley), Fred Carson (creature 2), Frank da Vinci (Brent), Roger Holloway (Roger Lemli), Pete Kellett (creature 3), Jeannie Malone (Yeoman), Eddie Paskey (Leslie), Frieda Rentie (Sciences crew woman 2)

Antagonist: The Eymorg

Responses:

'The story is completely bereft of the intelligence, plausibility and disciplined imagination that had characterized the series in its premiere season two years previous. It's as hollow and nonsensical as any given episode of **Lost In Space**.'

[Dennis Russell Bailey, Trekmovie.com, 14 June 2007]

'The problem isn't the story. The problem is almost everything else. The tone is far too silly for the series, and the actors are phoning in their performances.'

[Patrick J Mullen, Medium.com, 3 September 2020]

SYNOPSIS

A mysterious woman beams onto bridge of the Enterprise and stuns the entire crew, before examining each of them in turn. When they awaken, **Dr. McCoy** finds **Commander Spock** in sick bay with his brain surgically removed. Without his brain, Spock's body can be kept alive for no more than twenty-four hours.

In pursuit of the brain, the Enterprise follows the alien ship's ion trail to the Sigma Draconis system, and a frozen ice world. An all male group of natives attack the landing party but are repulsed, and a captured attacker warns **Captain Kirk** about the Others, 'the givers of pain and delight'.

McCoy beams down with Spock's body, which is able to walk independently only due to an electronic control device. The landing party travel underground in a lift, and encounter a woman named **Luma**, who seems to have the mentality of a child. Just before they are captured by the underground dwellers - the Others, a female dominated society who seem far more technically advanced than those on the surface - they hear Spock's voice via communicator.

Kara, the leader of the underground people is the woman who appeared on the Enterprise bridge and, presumably, took Spock's brain (though she claims not even to know what a brain is when questioned by Kirk). Eventually, she suggests they must mean **the Controller**, on whom the underground civilisation is dependent.

In spite of pain bands placed round their waists by the women, the landing party escapes and Spock's voice guides them to the control room where his brain is housed. Kara admits that the skills needed to remove a brain are not ones she has normally, but that they come from the **Teacher**, a machine accessed by a large headset, a remnant from a previous period in the planet's history, and that the knowledge provided lasts only three hours.

McCoy uses the Teacher to restore Spock's brain, even though to do so puts his own life at risk, but as time passes his new knowledge begins to fade, endangering Spock's life in turn. Fortunately, Spock himself is able to help after McCoy re-connects his speech centre.

Without their Controller, which will not run without Spock's brain, Kara fears for the future of her society. Kirk assures her that men and women can learn to survive together on the surface.

CHAPTER 1: TEASER

If I Only Had a Brain

11pm on Friday 20 September 1968, and across America the sense of disappointment for many **Star Trek** fans was all-consuming.

What we now call **The Original Series (TOS)** had returned for a third year, and as with the previous year's season opener[1], it was a story centred on the show's breakout character, Spock. Alas, this was to be no *Amok Time* (1967), and although the transmission of *Spock's Brain* won the ratings for the evening, beating the pilot movie of **Hawaii Five-O** (1968-80) with a 36% audience share[2], this would mark the beginning of the episode's notoriety, rightly or wrongly, which to this day it has been unable to shake off.

It didn't help that this was the first episode to air after the high profile 'Save **Star Trek**' Campaign' which had seen over 100,000[3] letters sent in to TV network NBC. As campaigner Doug Drexler shared: 'I was crushed by *Spock's Brain* when I saw it. I couldn't believe this was **my** show. What the hell had happened?'[4] This disappointment was not confined to the fans. In later years, the series leads and the producer joined in. From series lead William Shatner: 'Our first show that third season might have been a tribute to the NBC executives who so mishandled this show,'[5] to Leonard

---

[1] **TOS**: *Amok Time* (1967).
[2] Cushman, Marc, *These are the Voyages, TOS: Season Three*, p199.
[3] 'From early December to date, NBC has received 114,667 pieces of mail in support of **Star Trek**, and 52,151 in the month of February alone.' NBC press release, 4 March 1968.
[4] Cushman, *These are the Voyages, TOS: Season Three*, p200.
[5] Shatner, William with David Fisher, *Up Till Now*, pp132-133.

Nimoy: 'What we ended up with was an episode that was kind of a no-brainer. Not our best,'[6] to Producer Robert H Justman: 'I love 'em all, even *Spock's Brain*, which was possibly the worst one we ever made,'[7] the episode has gained a notoriety that has pushed it into popular culture in a way that few other episodes have.

A parody of *Spock's Brain* was featured in an episode of ABC's Sixties and Seventies-set comedy drama **The Wonder Years** (1988-93)[8] and it inspired the plot for adult movie *Sex Trek II: The Search for Sperm* (1991), though this time it was the Vulcan's penis rather than his brain that was taken by a sexy female thief. In 2004, Mike Carano directed a nine-week run of *Spock's Brain* at the Improv Irvine comedy club in California, performed nightly by a troupe of costumed actors[9]. Even an economics textbook gets in on the *Spock's Brain* debate, claiming:

> 'Contra Episode 61, even Spock's brain could not come close to running a modern economy. For this reason, some economists consider *Spock's Brain* to be the **worst Star Trek** episode ever.'[10]

Forget the fan and series stars' criticism – even economists give the episode a hard time!

---

[6] **Star Trek** Sci-Fi Channel Special Edition – 'Star Trek Insight: *Spock's Brain*'.
[7] Sci-Fi channel.
[8] *Just Between Me and You and Kirk and Paul and Carla and Becky* (1989).
[9] Nemecek, Larry, 'Licensed and Live: *Spock's Brain*: A Retro-Kitsch Hit for the Ages'.
[10] Cowe, Tyler and Alex Tabarrok, *Modern Principles: Macroeconomics*, p14.

So, what is it about *Spock's Brain*? Even the title is clunky; it's the only time in **TOS** that one of its main characters' names was used in an episode title, and it's positively screaming out for an exclamation mark to complete the B-movie connection. It has literally become the benchmark for poor episodes of **Star Trek**, the authors of book *Star Trek 101*[11] bestowing the *Spock's Brain Award* to the weakest episode of each **Star Trek** series. It has become synonymous with 'bad' or 'worst', possibly based as much on the name-recognition than the individual's knowledge of the episode itself. In **Friends'** (1994-2004) parlance, it's *The One Where a Space Babe Steals Spock's Brain*, and for many that is all they know about the episode, beyond recalling stills of Spock in his boiler suit.

Marj Dusay recalls meeting Majel Barrett, Gene Roddenberry's wife at a golf tournament in Palm Springs, and Barrett saying to her: 'Oh, you're the one who did *Spock's Brain*, the worst, stupidest, rottenest episode we ever did.'[12] It's a brutal putdown of the episode, aimed at someone who did nothing but act in the show, but it highlights the strength of opinion held about it.

But there's a lot more going on in *Spock's Brain* than quotable bad lines of dialogue and a remote-control Vulcan.

This study takes a closer look at the episode and unpicks what makes it so unpopular, revealing some darker, more distasteful aspects that you might not have considered. It will attempt to convince you that scratching beneath its label of shame reveals an hour of casual sexism, objectification and misogyny.

The original story outline and multiple drafts of the script highlight

---

[11] Erdmann, Terry J and Paula M. Block, *Star Trek 101*, p23.
[12] Jankiewicz, Pat, 'I Stole *Spock's Brain*', *Starlog* #51.

significant changes in the story's development and the point where the unsavoury aspects crept in. Gene Roddenberry's post-**TOS** work is also reviewed to predict whether his direct involvement with Season 3 might have led to a better episode, as well as charting how the 2250s and 2260s *Enterprise* (in movies and series) has been depicted post-**TOS**.

Where sexism is referenced, it will be in comparison to other **Star Trek** episodes and the show's ideals. Through 21st century eyes, it's a given that the depiction of women on the show is outdated and frequently offensive, so *Spock's Brain* is measured here relative to **TOS**' own standards, which frequently had been so much higher. **TOS** had already been so much more enlightened and better than *Spock's Brain*, though its progressive agenda could still be undermined by its stereotyping of women as domestics, love interests and window dressing for heterosexual men. This is a story of contradictions, of things said but not done, and things denied but there to be seen. It's a show that wants its cake and to eat it too, by preaching equality but skewing towards straight male fantasy.

References to 'men', 'male gaze', 'appealing to men', 'sexism', 'battle of the sexes', etc, in this work refer to straight cis males as they would have been understood by the US public at the time of original transmission in September 1968. The episode is not reviewed through the more enlightened contemporary lens which celebrates a far more inclusive view of gender, as evidenced in **Star Trek: Discovery**, for example.

Before beaming down to Dracaris VI to meet the Eymorgs, givers of pain and delight, some context from Leonard Nimoy: '*Spock's Brain*. A promising title and yet the mere mention of it sends shivers down the spine of most **Star Trek** fans. If you rank every episode from best to worst, this one would almost undoubtedly be at the bottom. Let's face it, the plot is silly, the acting is only passable. Altogether, not one of our best. But that said, however, let's give it a second chance. Forget the silliness and think about it from a pure science fiction standpoint. It's time we all took a fresh look at *Spock's Brain*.[13]

---

[13] 'Star Trek Insight: *Spock's Brain*'.

CHAPTER 2: NUMBER ONE AND THE YEOMAN

It Started so Well

It would be 25 years after **TOS** had finished its first run before a **Star Trek** series boasted a female main cast first officer (Major Kira Nerys in **Deep Space Nine**) and a further two before Captain Kathryn Janeway became the first main cast female captain, on **Voyager**[14]. When watching the poor depiction of women in *Spock's Brain*, we can at least take comfort with hindsight in knowing that things would eventually change for the better.

It would be easy to dismiss the portrayal of the Eymorgs by arguing that this was a common portrayal of women in the 1960s. And while it's true that there was considerable casual sexism at that time, when looking at the origins of **TOS**, we see that it started with strong foundations for women – one in particular – but that changes were introduced subsequent to the early pitches and pilot episode, weakening the desired depiction of sexual equality. If Number One had remained as the show's second-in-command, maybe we'd have seen a different interaction between the captain and his female subordinates. And if the crew members had been treated with more equality, maybe the visiting alien races, including the Eymorgs, would have been portrayed and managed differently.

---

[14] An unnamed non-main cast female captain appeared in *The Voyage Home* (1986) and Captain Phillipa Louvois in **TNG**'s *The Measure of a Man* (1989).

Number One: 'Almost mysteriously female'

TOS pilot episode *The Cage* (1965, but not broadcast in its original form until 1988) opens with Number One at the helm of the *Enterprise*. Played by Majel Barrett (though credited on-screen with her birth name M Leigh Hudec) the lieutenant commander takes commands from Captain Pike as they pick up a distress signal. Contemporary documents reveal how the show's female lead character was first pitched to the network. In the *Series Format*, under the summary of 'Other Cast Regulars, Number One is described as a 'glacierlike, efficient, female who serves as ship's Executive Officer.'[15] The fact that she doesn't have an actual name yet is of no great concern, as maybe it will be a running joke or thread in the subsequent stories.[16] The word 'glacierlike' is presumably a variant (or misspelling) of 'glacial', which if describing a woman typically means they are very beautiful and elegant, but do not show their feelings.[17]

Her character biography in the pitch document **Star Trek** *is...* gives us far more detail:

> 'Number One; this officer is female. Almost mysteriously female, in fact – slim and dark in a Nile Valley way, age uncertain, one of those women who will always look the same between years twenty and fifty. An extraordinarily efficient

---

[15] Whitfield and Roddenberry, *The Making of Star Trek*, p24. Although this book is credited to both, all quotations in this Archive are attributed to Whitfield unless otherwise indicated.

[16] When Spock tells her that her name is Una in **Short Treks**' *Q&A* (2019) she corrects him: 'That isn't a question, Ensign. My name is Number One.'

[17] Collins English Dictionary.

officer, Number One enjoys playing it expressionless, cool – is probably Robert April's [the original name for the *Enterprise* captain] superior in detailed knowledge of the multiple equipment systems, departments, and crew members aboard the vessel. When Captain April leaves the craft, Number One moves up to Acting Commander.'[18]

Already there are significant strengths attributed to her; she's efficient, she's cool (more akin to calm than glacial), is probably superior to the captain in her understanding of the ship, and is the acting commander while he's away. Surely a description of a first officer that **DS9**'s Kira would approve of, though the character's indeterminate age, and being 'slim and dark' seem less relevant here, the revision of her biography in a later draft of the document added 'space' so that she's now an 'efficient space officer' and substituted 'crew members' with 'personnel'.[19]

On balance, it still feels like a firm foundation on which to base a commanding character, even if the following description is included in the script: '...almost glacierlike in her imperturbability and precision. From time to time we'll wonder just how much female exists under the icy façade.'[20] The new, more positive connotation given to glacierlike now seems to imply that it's not a typical feminine quality, and that we might see some of that warmth as she thaws out across the series.

On-screen, Number One does indeed play it cool, calmly accepting Pike's directive that that she remains on the ship ('I have to leave the

---

[18] First Draft, dated 11 March 1964.
[19] Whitfield and Roddenberry, *The Making of Star Trek*, p29.
[20] Revised script, dated 20 November 1964, p3.

most experienced officer covering us,') though she looks crestfallen when Pike says: 'I just can't get used to having a woman on the bridge. No offence, Lieutenant. You're different of course.' Different, as in lacking in feminine qualities, or because he doesn't think of her sexually? It's not clear.

In *The Cage*, Number One demonstrates her knowledge and command by leading the engineering crew to blast through the Talosian lift doors and suggesting that they try transporting inside the rock formation. She also shows her humanity in her willingness to self-sacrifice when setting the 'laser' to overload – 'It's wrong to create a whole wave of humans to live as slaves.' She also displays her emotions by looking offended when Vina makes a jibe about her potential as a mate: 'You're no better choice. They'd have better luck crossing him with a computer.' And she looks flustered and embarrassed when the Keeper says 'The female you call Number One has the superior mind and would produce highly intelligent children. Although she seems to lack emotion, this is largely a pretence. She has often had fantasies involving you.' This is certainly a less glacial person than we were given to expect.

After they watched the pilot, network executives requested a number of changes, as Roddenberry explained.

> 'NBC recommended eliminating the character of Number One ... Audience tests of this character, after viewing the pilot, ranged from resentment to disbelief. ... Although **Star Trek** was a show about the 23rd Century, it was being viewed by a 20th Century audience – who resented the idea of a tough, strong-willed woman ("too domineering") as second-in-

command.'[21]

This version of events is disputed by Producer Herb Solow, who reported that NBC's feedback was 'We support the concept of a woman in a strong, leading role, but we have serious doubts as to Majel Barrett's ability to "carry" the show as its co-star.'[22] He concluded '...the NBC execs, for both financial and moral reasons, had always favoured a strong woman as the series star. They just didn't want Majel...'[23]

Whether NBC didn't like this strong woman or the married Roddenberry couldn't face recasting his then-girlfriend (later wife), TOS lead William Shatner contextualised the character in 1993. 'It's incredible to think that in 1964, Gene Roddenberry was sending one [a woman] into space in a position of utmost authority. Even today, a female character of Number One's intelligence, competence and power would meet with uneasy stares at any pitch meeting.'[24]

Yeoman Colt: 'very female, disturbingly so'

Number One didn't make it to the second pilot, let alone the series, many of her glacial qualities seemingly given to Mr Spock to calm him down after his shouty performances in *The Cage* and *Where No Man Has Gone Before* (1966). A different female character continued in the show, though she was more closely aligned to the sexist depiction of women that would lead to sexualised and 'available' characters like Kara and Luma in *Spock's Brain*.

---

[21] Whitfield and Roddenberry, *The Making of Star Trek*, p128.
[22] Solow and Justman, *Inside Star Trek*, p60.
[23] Solow and Justman, *Inside Star Trek*, p157.
[24] Shatner, William with Chris Kreshki, *Star Trek Memories*, p23.

In the **TOS** *Series Format*, a summary of 'Other Cast Regulars' features '...and uncomfortably lovely J M Colt, the Captain's Yeoman.'[25] Such sexist language immediately conjures up questions as to why someone might be uncomfortable in her presence. Played by Laurel Goodwin, her character name is not spoken onscreen or shown on the episode credits, and is derived purely from script or background sources.

Her more detailed character biography in the ***Star Trek*** pitch[26] describes:

> 'The Captain's Yeoman. Except for problems in naval parlance, Colt would be called a yeowoman; blonde and with a shape even a uniform cannot hide. She serves as Captain April's secretary, reporter, bookkeeper and undoubtedly wishes she could also serve him in more personal departments. She is not dumb; she **is** very female, disturbingly so.'

This is not a female character defined by her power or abilities, instead throwing up a number of troubling questions: why would she have to hide her body (shapely – because she is a woman?) under her uniform, why are her fantasies being second-guessed, and why is her femininity disturbing? The misogyny here displays a genuine fear/hatred of female-kind. Clarifying that she is not dumb is also telling. Might we have assumed otherwise because she is blonde, or because she is so very feminine?

In the revised version of the document[27], there are changes that both strengthen and weaken her character. She's no longer blonde and

---

[25] Whitfield and Roddenberry, *The Making of Star Trek*, p24.
[26] First Draft, 11 March 1964.
[27] Whitfield and Roddenberry, *The Making of Star Trek*, p30.

operates with efficiency (as if that needed to be spelt out), but instead of just having a shape that her uniform cannot hide, she has: 'a strip-queen figure,' thus sealing her fate as primarily a fantasy figure. Producer Herb Solow confirmed as much. 'Gene's version of the ship's yeoman role came straight out of old Hollywood movies: cute and shapely, and cute and bubbly, and cute and not too bright."[28]

In the episode script[29] she's described as: 'About twenty, she's pert and shapely, but carries herself with trained precision.'

William Shatner considered why Colt was written this way: 'It would be interesting to know if ... she was merely tossed into the mix in an astute attempt to appeal to the prurient interest of the cigar-chomping, upper middle-age network suits who generally read these proposals.'[30]

Colt's sexuality would be incorporated in the plot, the Keeper telling Pike that 'The other new arrival has considered you unreachable but now is realizing this has changed. The factors in her favour are youth and strength, plus unusually strong female drives.' Colt shifts uncomfortably on hearing this, but at the episode's conclusion still asks the captain, 'I was wondering... just curious, understand... who would have been Eve?', her vanity demanding to know whether it was she or Number One who would have been Pike's chosen mate.

---

[28] Solow and Justman, *Inside Star Trek*, p75.
[29] Revised version, 20 November 1964, p10.
[30] Shatner, *Star Trek Memories*, p24.

Yeoman Smith: 'A capable secretary and efficient dispenser of instant coffee'

Colt not make it to the second pilot either, although the character of a yeoman carried over. A different yeoman, Smith, was included in *Where No Man Has Gone Before*, played by model Andrea Dromm. Herb Solow explained 'Laurel Goodwin as Yeoman Colt fit Gene's vision for the first pilot, but she was swept away by the NBC broom.'[31]

The cover of the *NBC Advance Information Guide on 1966-67 Programming* brochure features a screaming Yeoman Smith hanging on to Kirk's arm. Her character synopsis clarifies that she's: '...easily the most popular member of Kirk's staff. A capable secretary and efficient dispenser of instant coffee, she also provides a welcome change of scenery for eyes that have spent long hours scanning the vast reaches of space.' Her role on the show is here galvanised – a combination of the sexist stereotype of a 'popular' and distracting woman with the stereotypical domestic skills of a kitchen maid, valet and general Girl Friday.

In the episode itself, she does little more than politely correct Kirk when he incorrectly addresses her as Jones, stand closely behind him on the Bridge with a worried look on her face, or hold navigator Gary Mitchell's hand when she's frightened. She has none of the agency of Number One, not serving any role other than as a domestic, or the damsel in distress to be saved by the men. 'Actually, it was a non-part,' Solow later remarked, adding that director James Goldstone overheard Roddenberry say, 'I'm hiring her [Andrea Domm] because I want to score with her.'[32] So small is the role that the character

---

[31] Solow and Justman, *Inside Star Trek*, p75.
[32] Solow and Justman, *Inside Star Trek*, p75.

plays in the episode, she's not even in the revised first draft script[33], only in the revised final draft[34], described similarly to J M Colt as: 'female, pert, early twenties.'

The episode's guest female lead, Sally Kellerman as Doctor Elizabeth Dehner, benefits from being given a professional role – Doctor of Psychiatry – but when responding to an inappropriate remark by Gary Mitchell, is bizarrely labelled by him as 'walking freezer unit,' a revision following NBC's objection to the word 'frigid'[35] and its negative sexual connotations. Here she's closer to the 'glacierlike' Number One than the 'popular' yeoman.

Yeoman Rand: 'treated co-equal with males of the same rank'

While both Yeomen Colt and Smith failed to make it to series, the role would survive again, recast as a new recruit, Janice Rand, played for eight episodes by Grace Lee Whitney. Her character is described in the **Star Trek** Writers/Directors Guide[36]:

> 'Whether Yeoman Rand or a new character provided by the writer, this female Yeoman serves Kirk as his combination Executive Secretary-Valet-Military Aide. As such, she is always capable, a highly professional career girl.'

A factual summary, the sexist qualities of Colt's and Smith's descriptions are encouragingly absent. It continues:

> 'As with all female crewmen aboard, during duty hours she is

---

[33] Dated 27 May 1965.
[34] Dated 8 July 1965.
[35] Cushman, *These are the Voyages: TOS Season Three*, p82.
[36] Third Revision, 17 April 1967.

treated co-equal with males of the same rank, and the same level of efficient performance is expected. The Yeoman often carries a small over-the-shoulder case, a tricorder, about the size of a small handbag, which is also an electronic recorder-camera-sensor combination, immediately available to the Captain should he be away from his Command Console.'

This second paragraph is more disappointing, the implication being that outside of duty hours she is **not** treated as an equal. And why the need to clarify that while she's being treated as an equal, she's expected to be as equally efficient as her male peers? It seems to be addressing the sexist notion that females aren't as efficient as males, unless they're held accountable.

In her autobiography, Whitney recalled how the part was sold to her. 'Gene Roddenberry's original vision of the show's chemistry was built around a nucleus of four characters – Kirk, Spock, McCoy, and Rand.'[37] She continued 'The Kirk-Rand relationship asks the question, "How can you put an attractive female crewmember aboard ship with an attractive male crewmember and not expect nature to take its course?"'[38] and that: 'It was a sexy part, with lots of possibilities.'[39]

Kirk expressed his frustration at being looked after by Rand in sexist terms.

KIRK

When I get my hands on the Headquarters genius that assigned me a female yeoman...

---

[37] Whitney, Grace Lee, *The Longest Trek: My Tour of the Galaxy*, p10.
[38] Whitney, *The Longest Trek*, p75.
[39] Whitney, *The Longest Trek*, p72.

MCCOY

What's the matter Jim, don't you trust yourself?[40]

KIRK

I've already got a female to worry about. Her name's the *Enterprise*.[41]

Rand features prominently as the object of Charlie's affections in *Charlie X* (1966), is subjected to a sexual assault in *The Enemy Within* (1966) and drawn to the protection of Kirk in *The Naked Time* (1966), *Balance of Terror* (1966) and *Miri* (1966). While not of the seniority of Number One, she was ostensibly the show's initial female lead, gaining more screen time than Uhura, and then Whitney's agent informed her that she would be leaving the show. 'Apparently, they think that Captain Kirk needs to be free to have these affairs with other women on all these different planets,' she explained, adding, 'so, for me to be dropped from the show was a major shake-up – a sudden disruption of the chemical balance of the show.'[42] It's disappointing if the reason for her departure was indeed to give Kirk more opportunities for romance, as Roddenberry was trying to develop the character, 'trying to work out additional duties for the Captain's Yeoman, fill out her role a bit, plus give her some landing party duties where we need her on a planet'.[43] Whitney believed that the unnamed executive who she alleges sexually assaulted her at the studio had a say in the decision: 'I have always believed that

---

[40] In subsequent episode **TOS**: *The Enemy Within* (1966), Kirk is shown that he cannot in fact be trusted with Rand.
[41] **TOS**: *The Corbomite Maneuver* (1966).
[42] Whitney, *The Longest Trek*, p9.
[43] Whitfield and Roddenberry, *The Making of Star Trek*, p169.

The Executive had me removed from *Star Trek* because he didn't want to be reminded of what he did to me that night.[44]

There would always be limitations to her role as Kirk's valet-secretary. There was a built-in, uneven distribution of power, with Kirk, as her superior, having the upper hand. Writers never fully developed the role, as witness lines like 'I'm upset, so upset. Back on the ship, I used to try to get you to look at my legs. Captain, look at my legs.'[45] In this case, like the other members of the landing party, Rand has been infected by a disease and her legs are blotchy. As written, dialogue played up her female vanity, affording Kirk the opportunity to hug her and reassert his dominance. Summarising her role on the ship, Whitney said 'I tell everybody I was a space geisha!'

Rand's departure allowed a revolving door of female love interests for Kirk. Writer Karin Blair has argued that 'in almost every episode we have a different female guest star, which usually guarantees that the character she portrays is alien and disposable. Most often she dies, disappears, or remains at the service of a father figure.' Blair continued that most of these women are a projection of Kirk's anima – 'the internalised image of ideal femininity he carries inside him ... conceived as embodiments of male fantasies, they cannot encounter men on the axis of sex on an equal and potentially maturing basis.'[46]

Lieutenant Uhura: 'a desirable and attractive young lady'

After Rand left the *Enterprise*, she was succeeded by a series of 10

---

[44] Whitney, *The Longest Trek*, p15.
[45] **TOS**: *Miri* (1966).
[46] Blair, Karin, *Meaning in Star Trek*, pp126, 129, 140.

yeomen, brought in to serve the story as required. Two female characters were present from the beginning of the series, however, and would last all three seasons – Lieutenant Uhura[47] and Nurse Christine Chapel. The communications officer would go on to appear in 66 episodes of **TOS**. Her character description in the *Star Trek Writers/Directors Guide*[48] states that she is:

> 'played by attractive young actress Nichelle Nichols. Uhura was born in the United States of Africa. Quick and intelligent, she is a highly efficient officer and expert in all ships systems relating to communications. Uhura is also a warm, highly female female off duty. She is something of a favourite in the Recreation Room during off duty hours, too, because she sings – old ballads as well as the newer space ballads – and she can do an impersonation at the drop of a communicator.'

Apart from the unnecessary qualification that Nicholls is attractive, this is a solid portrait of her character, initially focusing on her efficiency and the range of her professional skills. Regrettably, we need to be told that she is a highly 'female female off-duty,' which begs the question why she cannot be a 'female female' while **on** duty, and what those qualities are. Significantly. Nicholls played Uhura as a strong woman.

'When you're out in space, in a dangerous situation where the ship might be blown up at any time, you're not going to have some female that says, 'Ooooh Captain, save me, save me!'' she explained to David

---

[47] Her first name Nyota is only mentioned on screen for the first time in *Star Trek* (2009), although created for the tie-in stories to *The 'rath of Khan* in 1982.
 'rd Revision, 17 April 1967.

Gerrold in 1975. 'All those female things, delicate how-are-we-going-to-do-it-without-you-Captain things... She knows that whole panel and all of a sudden she's supposed to become little lady milquetoast? Ridiculous!'[49]

While she displays strength and skill at her station, she was still being described as: 'a desirable and attractive young lady, and a highly able starship officer, considered by Captain Kirk fully as capable as any lieutenant abroad.'[50] Regrettably, her looks and desirability define her ahead of her abilities, and the point is made that she's as capable as any other lieutenant on the vessel – should it be inferred that the comparison is with males?

Nurse Christine Chapel: 'desperately in love with Mr Spock...'

Of the qualities that define Christine Chapel, played by Majel Barrett in 25 episodes of **TOS** and *The Motion Picture* (1979)[51], strength is not one the most obvious. Producer Robert Justman would go as far as to say: 'Nurse Chapel was a wimpy, badly written, and ill-conceived character, all she did was stand around and pine for Mister Spock, much the same as Yeoman Rand did for Captain Kirk'.[52] In the **Star Trek** Writers/Directors Guide,[53] she's described as:

'Dr McCoy's Head Nurse, a skilled Surgical Assistant, as near to a professional confidant as the irascible "Bones" McCoy is

---

[49] Gerrold, David, *The World of Star Trek*, p115.
[50] Whitfield and Roddenberry, *The Making of Star Trek*, p252.
[51] She cameos in a non-speaking role in *Star Trek IV: The Voyage Home* (1986).
[52] Solow and Justman, *Inside Star Trek*, p225.
[53] Third Revision, 17 April 1967.

likely to have. That relationship never transgresses onto the personal and an unspoken bond is the fact that she, too, is in a Starfleet Service because of a tragic romance. Although she herself holds several university degrees in Research Medicine, she has found a measure of contentment in this life as a Starfleet Nurse and wanderer.'[54]

The confirmation that her relationship with McCoy never oversteps into 'personal' is a curious one, pre-supposing that if a man and woman work closely together then this is likely to happen. The real 'tragedy' here is that Chapel, a highly qualified woman, has had to take a perceived step back from what she might have achieved and settled for the compromise of being a nurse. Under different circumstances, she might have been the ship's chief medical officer, the original Beverley Crusher, and it isn't until *The Motion Picture* (1979) that her qualification and title of Doctor are confirmed.

The back story alluded to in her biography is confirmed in *What Are Little Girls Made of?* (1966), with on-screen confirmation that, following the disappearance of her fiancé Dr Kirby five years prior, she had given up a career in bio-research to sign on aboard the *Enterprise*. Having been traced to planet Exo III, Korby is discovered to have transplanted his personality into an android before killing himself. Chapel understandably opts to remain on the *Enterprise*.

We're also told that 'like many women aboard, Christine is desperately in love with Mr Spock...'[55] While under the influence of the virus from Psi 2000 in *The Naked Time*, she expresses these feelings towards him: '...I'm in love with you, Mr Spock. You, the

---

[54] Third Revision, 17 April 1967.
[55] Whitfield and Roddenberry, *The Making of Star Trek*, p254.

human Mr Spock, the Vulcan Mr Spock... I love you. I don't know why, but I love you. I do love you just as you are. Oh, I love you.' In spite of this declaration, this remains an unrequited love, occasionally referenced in the series.

Curiously, the **TOS** executives were in a state of denial about how women were being used in their show, as evidenced when they challenged would-be writers or directors[56] to identify why a sample description of a storyline 'tease' would be out of place in a future episode. A bolt of photon energy plasma hits the ship and 'Kirk puts his arms about his lively Yeoman, comforting and embracing her as they wait for what seems like certain death.' And why was that scenario incorrect? 'Because it's unbelievable. The Captain would not hug a pretty Yeoman on the bridge of his vessel.' Except that's exactly what he did with Yeoman Rand in *Balance of Terror*, which is conveniently forgotten here.

The description of the various yeomen did not suggest equality on the ship – certainly none of the male characters have biographies that focus on their physical appearance or sexual availability. Roddenberry recalls his struggle with the network to create that equality:

> 'in those days we had the *Enterprise* 50 percent men, 50 percent women.' The network visited the set and raised a concern about the gender split. He said, "Because, don't you see, it will make it look like there's a lot of fooling around going on up there." We had a huge argument, he went away,

---

[56] *Star Trek Writers/Directors Guide*, Third Revision, 17 April 1967, excerpted in Whitfield and Roddenberry, *The Making of Star Trek*, pp324-326.

> came back a week later and said... "You can have 30% women." I thought "...30% healthy young women should be able to handle the ship..."'[57]

A compromise in numbers, but also a perpetuation of a sexist attitude that the 30% of women can 'handle' the 70% men.

The show was missing a strong female who could have stood alongside her contemporaries in other network shows. Of the yeomen, the **TOS** producers would lament that

> '...they were the antithesis of the actresses starring in the other dramatic television series of that era: Barbara Bain (**Mission: Impossible**), Amanda Blake (**Gunsmoke**), Barbara Anderson (**Ironside**), Stephanie Powers (**The Girl from U.N.C.L.E.**), and of course Barbara Stanwyck (**The Big Valley**), all playing characters of substantial independence and distinction.'[58]

Number One could have filled that role, but this wasn't to be.

Second-wave feminism and professional roles

A new wave of feminism was emerging in mid-60s America, riding the wave of Betty Friedan's best-seller *The Feminine Mystique*. She argued that: 'A woman today has been made to feel freakish and alone and guilty if, simply, she wants to be more than her husband's wife.'[59] This was the myth of the feminine mystique; that the woman was content to stay at home, being fully dependent on her husband.

---

[57] *Inside Star Trek*, 'The *Enterprise* Runs Aground', Side B, Track 1.
[58] Justman and Solow, *Inside Star Trek*, p226.
[59] Friedan, Betty, *The Feminine Mystique*, p76.

In 1964, she expanded on the Feminine Mystique, as it applied to television:

> 'it defines women solely in sexual terms, as man's wife, mother, love object, dishwasher, and general server of physical needs, and never in human terms, as a person herself. It glorifies woman's only purpose as the fulfilment of her 'femininity' – through sexual passivity, loving service of husband and children, and dependence on man for all decisions in the world outside of her home.' [60]

Career women were frowned upon, and they struggled to find the same job opportunities as males, certainly not at the same salaries. Instead, they were encouraged to fit the homemaker mould/stereotype. In 1964, MGM executive producer Norman Felton explained why women were infrequent leads or weren't portrayed as holding careers. 'For a woman to make decisions, to triumph over anything, would be most unpleasant, dominant, masculine. After all, most women are housewives... [and] would react against a woman who succeeded at anything.'[61]

But this was now 1968, and women watching **TOS** at the time of original transmission could possibly have been inspired by seeing female characters in professional roles such as doctor, attorney, historian or psychiatrist. Equally, they probably rolled their eyes at the sexualised alien races like the simple, matriarchal Eymorgs, or the coffee-dispensing and file-carrying yeomen. When challenged in a letter by Margaret M. Bailey from New Jersey in 1975 as to whether

---

[60] Friedan, Betty, 'Television and the Female Mystique,' in *TV Guide: The First 25 Years*, p93.
[61] Friedan, 'Television and the Female Mystique,' p96.

he thought that **TOS** was male chauvinistic by the standards of the mid-70s, Gene Roddenberry agreed:

> 'Yes, by today's standards, indeed it was. We didn't use women as strongly as we might have. We did have women lieutenants, women attorneys. We often fell into the trap of making the captain's secretary-valet – the yeoman – a woman. I think if we did begin today, we would start off more advanced than we were able to at the time.'[62]

But before we overly praise the show for at least having some professional women, remember that their depiction was typically of flawed people who were dissatisfied with their work, or quickly dropped the desire to be a career woman and instead fell into the arms of a charmer or flatterer. Look how easily Archaeology and Anthropology Officer Lieutenant Palamas is wooed by Apollo and abandons her professional role, wanting to become a goddess in *Who Mourns for Adonais?* (1967) or Lieutenant Marla McGivers, ship's historian, falls under the charm of Khan in *Space Seed* (1967). And if a new yeoman featured in an episode, she would typically abandon her post or professionalism – Yeoman Burrows fantasising about becoming a princess in *Shore Leave* (1966) and Yeoman Ross being enchanted by Trelane in *The Squire of Gothos* (1967), for instance.

Those women who were taking comfort from the optimism of a future where they could achieve their career goals, were watching their dreams being eroded through the depiction of frail women, who, as written, turned their backs on hard-fought career achievements and stepped back into society-approved stereotypes.

---

[62] Sackett, Susan, *Letters to Star Trek*, pp64-66.

Admittedly, it was still a step up from much contemporary TV fare where, as Gail Collins noted: 'you'd have thought that married women who worked were limited to a handful of elementary school teachers and the unlucky wives of sharecroppers and drunkards.'[63]

The final episode of **TOS** was *Turnabout Intruder* (1969) featuring Doctor Janice Lester, whose hatred of her own womanhood leads to the loss of her career. Perhaps even more depressing, though, is the exchange between Kirk and McCoy in *Who Mourns for Adonais?* where the doctor discusses Mr Scott's blossoming relationship with Lt Caroline Palamas.

> 'I'm not sure she thinks he's the right man [for her]... On the other hand, she's a woman. All woman. One day she'll find the right man and off she'll go, out of the service.'

If any comment in **TOS** encapsulates the show at its most sexist, this might be it. Not only is Marla a woman, she is 'all woman',

But luckily, there's an escape, in the form of marriage, which means that she would leave the service, presumably to stay at home and happily bring up children. Gail Collins said that marriage on TV 'created the impression that once married, a woman literally never left her house. Even if the viewers knew that this really wasn't true, many did accept the message that when matrimony began, working outside the home ended.'[64]

TOS might have been set in the 2260s, but it was very much grounded in the 1960s. Gene Roddenberry confirmed as much:

---

[63] Collins, Gail, *When Everything Changed: The Amazing Journey of American Women from 1960 to the Present*, p16.
[64] Collins, *When Everything Changed,* p15.

> 'Also, we can't ignore the fact that I was playing to a 1964-1966 audience, with a large group that would enjoy seeing women in a setting not too different from what was the norm **then** and would be pulled close to the show by seeing those things... Would I change that? I think not a great deal, although we talked about having more women around and giving them better assignments.'[65]

Another, more sinister, and less well-known, inequality for women in **TOS** was the proposed use of birth control. In the real-world, the first oral contraceptive pill became available in the United States in 1960, though it took cases like 1965's *Griswold v. Connecticut*[66] for the Supreme Court to rule that married couples have a Constitutional right to privacy that included the right to use birth control. However, millions of unmarried women in certain states were still denied the pill at that time. Surely, a science fiction show set two centuries in the future would offer up a world where women had total control of their lives, careers, and their bodies? Sadly not.

As explained in *The Making of **Star Trek***, though never featured on screen, 'Birth control would be mandatory for unmarried females...'. Just let that settle in for a moment. 'A woman found to be pregnant would be given her choice of a medical discharge or rotation to a shore base for the remainder of her pregnancy.' The rationale is that 'science recognises that the known, as well as the unknown, difficulties of pregnancy and birth in space makes the practice of birth control in some form completely necessary.'[67]

---

[65] Sackett, *Letters to Star Trek*, pp64-66.
[66] Griswold v. Connecticut (1965).
[67] Whitfield & Roddenberry, *The Making of Star Trek*, p207.

So, while the viewer is expected to believe that technology exists where a person can be beamed between two locations, bodies can be split into two, or even a Vulcan's brain can be removed on board ship without damaging it, pregnancy and birth were just a stretch too far for 23rd century science.

CHAPTER 3: THE THEISS TITILLATION THEORY

Dressed to Thrill

One of the problems with *Spock's Brain* is that the alien female (Eymorg) costumes don't hit the mark. Before examining why they're impractical, too obvious, too sexualised and parodic, we should contextualise what had gone before to bring the show up to this point, and indeed why the costumes had been so much better.

Ask someone to break down the characteristics of a typical **TOS** episode and it's likely to include 'alien women in sexy costume' or some similar variation in there. These exotic vestments were courtesy of the series' costume designer William 'Bill' Ware Theiss, who would fulfil this role for the series' three season run and make them an essential ingredient of the series.

William Shatner would observe that 'even within our first handful of episodes, Theiss had begun his series-long habit of keeping our guest actresses chilly... and nearly naked.'[68] The effectiveness is put down to what would be known as:

> 'the "Theiss Titillation Theory". According to Bill's theory, the degree to which a costume is considered sexy is directly dependent upon how accident-prone it appears to be... if it [the bikini] looks as if it might suddenly slip and something is in danger of accidental disclosure, then it suddenly becomes terribly titillating and sexy.'[69]

---

[68] Shatner, *Star Trek Memories*, p86.
[69] Whitfield and Roddenberry, *The Making of Star Trek*, p360.

One frequently cited example is Leslie Parrish's revealing pink chiffon outfit for *Who Mourns for Adonais?* where the front of the dress is held up by the weight of the train. Sherry Jackson's crossover halterneck and trouser combo worn by android Andrea in *What Are Little Girls Made Of?* is another example of the designer's ingenuity. 'Bill and Gene Roddenberry and myself... all three of us were designing that outfit. It was like some mechanical engineering job to make it work.'[70]

TOS gained a reputation for using revealing costumes in its shows, Theiss' costume designs permitted the actresses to show as much leg, breast and skin as possible, while attempting to adhere to the dictates of NBC's Broadcast Standards Department, the network censors.'[71]

After Theiss designed the costume for Vina as an Orion slave in *The Cage*, the network provided the feedback of 'too erotic'.[72] One person who would show particular interest in the female costumes for the show's pilot was Gene Roddenberry, whose 'penchant for unusual female costume design was fulfilled as he personally checked out the skimpy, diaphanous costumes worn by Susan Oliver'[73] Nichelle Nicholls reflected on Roddenberry's costume preferences. He 'liked beautifully gowned women, and he reflected that and insisted on it. You saw the little openings here, there, the cleavage there, they were dressed to the hilt with grey paint. They were still very sensuous wardrobes for women.'[74] Given all of this,

---

[70] StarTrek.com Staff, 'Catching up with TOS Android Andrea'.
[71] Solow and Justman, *Inside Star Trek,* p28.
[72] Solow and Justman, *Inside Star Trek,* pxviii.
[73] Solow, and Justman, *Inside Star Trek,* p39.
[74] Unknown, 'Interview: Nichelle Nichols – Your Costume'.

and the fact that Theiss had set the 'alien female costume' template with Vina from the outset in *The Cage*, what is so wrong with the Eymorg costumes?

At the most basic level, they lack credibility; they just don't make sense. Consider for a moment how the Eymorg society operates. The viewer is not given a lot to work with in the transmitted episode, though, as discussed in chapter 5, previous drafts shed more light on this female-led civilisation. The Eymorgs (female) lure the Morgs (male) down to their underground home by enticing them into a cave that contains food, furs, clubs, knives, hatchets and tools. When entering the cave, the Morgs spring the trap, the cave descends, and the occupants are overcome by previously-captured Morgs who are controlled by pain belts. These new captives are subdued, given pain belts too and then encouraged to breed with their Eymorg mistresses to keep the race going. We don't see any babies or children or find out what happens to the male babies, and the whole process is repeated when further propagation is required.

So why are they dressed so provocatively? They don't lure the Morgs themselves, they rely on tools and food. There's no obvious reason for these women to be dressed like this, in these impractical, and presumably uncomfortable costumes, other than to serve as window dressing to the story. Is there a lesbian subject here – that the clothing has been designed by and for other women to enjoy? The clothes would also need a degree of skill for their production. Presumably the Eymorgs periodically download this knowledge from the Teacher when clothing stocks run low?

The reality is more likely aligned to the wish of adding some sex appeal to the story and by upping the 'pain and delight' aspects of these dominant women by making them look like dominatrices. The thigh-high leather boot has long been associated with the dominatrix, her whip and bondage gear here being replaced by wrist and belt gadgets that dispense intense pain.

The characters are objectivised as sex objects, dressed up in a male's version of what they think the femmes should look like. Gene Roddenberry saw no harm in this treatment of women: 'I think there's nothing wrong with using women as sex symbols... as long as that's not the **only** way you're using women. If you're using them to the exclusion of their minds and attitudes and abilities and so on, that would be different.'[75]

Marj Dusay, who played Eymorg leader Kara was thrilled with the role.

> 'I remember reading the [casting] breakdown and seeing, "She runs an underground bevy of women who control men with pleasure and pain." I thought, "Whoop-de-doo, this is for me!"' The clothes did present certain challenges, though. 'When they fitted that costume on me, I said, "Oh, my Lord!" I couldn't sit in it, because if I sat down, the straps on the dress would collapse and it wouldn't look right. So I was never shot sitting down.[76] Those costumes were made for stomping, not sitting!' As an alien queen, 'I had all my drones with me, all these other nymphettes running around in these little costumes, but I was the leader of the band. I thought that halfway through the episode we should have broken into a

---

[75] Sackett, *Letters to Star Trek*, p65.
[76] In fact, Kara **is** shown sitting down during the episode, though behind a desk.

rock number, because we looked like a Sixties girl group!'[77]

This highlights another issue – the clothing doesn't look credible because it's more akin to what a 60s girl band, singer or backing singers might wear on stage. It's not a stretch to imagine Nancy Sinatra singing 'These Boots are Made for Walking' (1965) while wearing Kara's boots, or even **The Avengers'** Honor Blackman singing about these 'Kinky Boots' (1964) with her **Avengers** co-star Patrick Macnee. It's partly because they are so theatrical and overstated that these items pull us out of the episode's already-fragile credibility.

To be clear, these weren't the most provocative female fashions seen on **TOS**, but they do feel like some of the least subtle. This combination is not glamorous or elegant, it's fantasy fetish wear.

The rise of the miniskirt

In response to a fan letter of 30 September 1975, on the question whether the miniskirts worn by the female crew members were impractical, Roddenberry said:

> 'That may be so. Incidentally, we didn't take our miniskirts for the miniskirt craze. The miniskirt craze came in about a year after we had designed them. And I think there should be a little bow to Bill Theiss, our costume designer, who made those costumes very, very effective for women as well as for men.'[78]

While Theiss may have popularised the miniskirt within the show, it's disingenuous of Roddenberry to claim credit here on behalf of Theiss for the wider use of the garment – London-based designer Mary

---

[77] Jankiewicz, Pat, 'I Stole *Spock's Brain*', *Starlog* #51.
[78] Sackett, *Letters to Star Trek*, p65.

Quant and Parisian André Courrèges had been promoting the miniskirt in their fashion designs as early as 1964, and prior to that the miniskirt had been a sci-fi staple since the 1940s. Artist Earle K. Bergey, had been painting colourful covers for pulp magazines including *Thrilling Wonder Stories*, *Startling Stories* and *Captain Future* since 1940, his images featuring exotic females in metallic bikinis, conical bras and miniskirts[79].

Samuel Peeples, the writer of *Where No Man Has Gone Before*, said of Gene Roddenberry's research for **TOS**: 'I have a collection of science fiction magazines, probably one of the most complete around. He and I waded through them, and photographed some of the covers, and we discussed every element of what he was doing.'[80] Perhaps these were the images that were passed on to the costume designer, as we're told that: 'Theiss utilized the pictures of scantily clad women in pulp science-fiction magazines like *Amazing Stories* and *Astounding Stories* as his point of departure.'[81]

On screen, Carol Hughes had been sporting a miniskirt as Dale Arden in 1940 for the 12-part film serial **Flash Gordon Conquers the Universe**, while the eponymous *Fire Maidens of Outer Space* (1956) wore minidresses, Anne Francis' Altaira Morbius in *Forbidden Planet* (1956) wore a minidress, as did the Venusians in *Missile to the Moon* (1958), whose outfits could be described as proto-Starfleet. On TV's **Space Patrol** (1950-1955), Carol Carlisle was wearing a red minidress over 15 years before Uhura and Rand. Without labouring this point even further, the sci-fi mini was nothing new, another reason why

---

[79] See, for instance, covers of *Thrilling Wonder Stories*, Spring 1944 and *Startling Stories*, Winter 1946.
[80] Asherman, Allan, *The Star Trek Interview Book*, pp114-115.
[81] Solow and Justman, *Inside Star Trek*, p28.

the Eymorg costume doesn't impress. It's a tired, over-used design, suggesting a lack of imagination, or possibly time and money. Many of Theiss' designs have an otherworldly chic that adds to the futuristic drama, while the *Spock's Brain* Eymorg get-up feels like it could more easily be picked up off the rack at a BDSM store.

Of the Eymorg costume, the miniskirt is the least novel component, having been a staple of the female Starfleet uniform in **TOS** (albeit as a minidress variant) since the show went to series. In both *The Cage* and *Where No Man Has Gone Before* the *Enterprise* crewmembers wear unisex uniforms of top and trousers, although the latter for the women were tailored to be more figure-hugging.

The Making of Star Trek chronicles that Bill Theiss '...was immediately put to work redesigning the costumes. It had been decided that instead of slacks, the women would wear the short mini-skirt uniforms they now wear.'[82] Was this a retrograde step for the show, the rising of the hems being a cynical triumph of titillation over realism? The series' female leads didn't think so. In fact, Grace Lee Whitney claims that it was her idea. She recalled telling Roddenberry: '"you're covering up my best part – my dancers' legs. Rand should wear a skirt – a short one!" He loved the idea but it wasn't **his** idea or Bill Theiss' idea, although it **was** their idea as to how short that skirt turned out.'[83]

Nichelle Nicholls wore a red miniskirt as Lieutenant Uhura throughout the three seasons of **TOS**, and had no reservations about the above-the-knee costume:

> 'I was wearing them on the street. What's wrong with wearing

---

[82] Whitfield and Roddenberry, *The Making of Star Trek*, p262.
[83] Cushman, *These are the Voyages: TOS Season One*, p121.

them in the air? I wore 'em on airplanes. It was the era of the miniskirt. Everybody wore miniskirts... It amazes me that people still make some remark about "the revealing". They revealed nothing. I had long black stockings on and boots up to my knees and the skirts and panties on and a skirt that gave you freedom to move in... It amazes me because everything is more revealing today on the street than those costumes.'[84]

Mary Quant noted: 'I think the Sixties mini was the most self-indulgent, optimistic fashion ever devised: young, liberated and exuberant — and the beginning of women's lib.'[85] The wearing of a miniskirt in the mid-1960s was more than just a fashion statement, it was a political statement of intent. Women were demonstrating they could dress as they pleased, without needing the approval of the patriarchy, the miniskirt being a key component of their armoury.

In her autobiography, Nicholls continues:

'In later years, especially as the women's movement took hold in the seventies, people began to ask me about my costume. Some thought it "demeaning" for a woman in the command crew to be dressed so sexily. It always surprised me because I never saw it that way. After all, the show was created in the age of the miniskirt, and the crew woman's uniforms were very comfortable. Contrary to what many may think today, no one really saw it as demeaning back then. In fact, the miniskirt was a symbol of sexual liberation. More to the point, in the twenty-third century, you are respected for your abilities

---

[84] 'Interview: Nichelle Nichols - Your Costume'.
[85] Quant, Mary, quoted in 'Mary Quant – Lights, Camera, Action, Mini Skirts are Back!'.

regardless of what you do or do not wear.'[86]

Nichols continues: 'she was a **female** female[87]. I mean, she had legs and boobs and high cheekbones and a little waistline and different hairdos. I don't think she's diminished by a short skirt, boots and jade earrings.'[88]

Zoe Saldana would later play Uhura in a red minidress in *Star Trek* (2009) and stated that 'the dress Uhura wears was a crucial element that defined her in the series, so it helped quickly familiarise audiences with her.'[89] It had transcended being a reflection of a contemporary fashion item; instead of the iconic 'little black dress', Uhura had her little red dress.

Nicholls and Whitney continue to defend their costumes in later interviews, The design choice may still have been sexist and exploitative, but the actors just chose to weaponise it. Whether an, or just having fun, example of female vanity, building up their own profiles while competing for the limelight away with their male co-stars. at times they would even compete with themselves. Whitney reported 'Nichelle used to let her skirt sneak up a bit while sat at the communications station. That was no accident. She wasn't going to be 'out-legged' by me.'[90]

But as the women were literally no longer 'wearing the pants' in the relationship, was there still parity between the sexes? Can the same

---

[86] Nichols, Nichelle, *Beyond Uhura*, p169.
[87] This quote echoes her character description in the *Star Trek Writers/Directors Guide*: '...a warm, highly female female off duty.'
[88] Lowry, Brian, 'The Songs of Uhura', *Starlog* #116.
[89] Cotta Vaz, Mark. *Star Trek: The Art of the Film*, p127.
[90] Cushman, *These are the Voyages: TOS Season One*, p121.

argument be used for the Eymorg costumes in *Spock's Brain*? Have we got it wrong, and the costumes are an expression of the rise of feminism – the right for a woman to dress how she wants?

The Starfleet minidress continued in **TAS**, but would be gone by the time of *The Motion Picture*, with male and female crew members wearing unisex uniforms. The authors of *The Making of Star Trek: The Motion Picture* contextualised the change. 'Fashion tastes had changed since the sixties – the miniskirt female costumes, so exciting ten years ago, would almost certainly be condemned in the seventies as sexist.'[91]

The unisex uniform was taken to the next stage in **The Next Generation** with Bill Theiss' unisex minidress garment, the spandex skant, being the 'logical development, given the total equality of the sexes presumed to exist in the 24th century.'[92] Thiess confirmed that 'having the actresses and actors both in skirts was to diffuse any sexist accusations that might have been associated with designs from the old show.'[93] The skant was used primarily by background actors, with male crewmembers wearing one in *Encounter at Farpoint* (1987), *Haven* (1987), *Where No One Has Gone Before* (1987), *Conspiracy* (1988), and *11001001* (1988). After frequent use in Season 1, it was only worn by female crew (with black trousers) in Season 2's *The Child* (1988), *The Outrageous Okona* (1988), *The Schizoid Man* (1989), and *Samaritan Snare* (1989), and in flashbacks during *All Good Things...* (1994).

---

[91] Sackett, Susan and Gene Roddenberry, *The Making of Star Trek: The Motion Picture*, p124.
[92] Reeves-Stevens, Judith and Garfield Reeves-Stevens, *The Art of Star Trek*, p88.
[93] Block, Paula M and Terry J Erdmann, *Star Trek Costumes*, p112.

Robert Blackman began working as costume designer for **Star Trek** with **TNG** Season 3 and explains why his designs for female characters were demurer:

> 'The notion of woman has changed since then. It's not that women are no longer sexual images, but we have to also depict them as something more than that, because they are. You know, in the mid-60s to 70s, it was **Barbarella**, it was Barbie, it was Babe time. But we can't in full honesty, and in modern thought process, do that.'[94]

Eymorg couture

Having identified what was wrong with the uninspired and overly sexualised Eymorg costumes, we have to wonder how it happened. With over 50 episodes of **TOS** under his belt at the time, Theiss knew how to design a female alien costume. Was he uninspired, tired or lacking in time and money? Maybe a little of all of these.

From the beginning, Theiss would be 'continually fighting the battle of time and budget. While he may have as much as two weeks in which to design and execute a costume, he frequently has five days or less.'[95] The reality was that 'some motion picture costumes will cost thousands of dollars apiece, while most **Star Trek** costumes will cost tens of dollars apiece.'[96] With these limited resources, Theiss was often up against it, resorting to running a 'sweatshop'.

'For Season 3, the budget had dropped per episode from Season 2's

---

[94] Unknown, 'Interview: Bob Blackman – Babes in space?'
[95] Whitfield and Roddenberry, *The Making of Star Trek*, p355.
[96] Whitfield and Roddenberry, *The Making of Star Trek*, p358.

$187,500 to $178,500[97]. This reduced budget also had to take into account an increase in salaries for its cast and general inflation of 4.19%[98] meaning that departments took an even bigger hit than the overall budget drop of just under 5% suggested. Maybe this is one of the reasons why the costumes in *Spock's Brain* are not Theiss' finest work. Less money, less time, something had to give, and maybe this was the episode to take the hit.

In television series, an episode is often required to subsidise another's over-run, thus reducing its budget even further. Concessions were being made on Season 3 to reduce costs – less location shooting, fewer guest stars – and cheaper, more basic, or less imaginative costumes would be one solution. But in an unexpected turn of events, we discover that despite: 'the new sets and an increased number of extras, stunt people, and props, the production finished $3,676 under budget.'[99]

What's disappointing is that the costumes in *Spock's Brain* fall short of the series' desire that 'The clothing must appear different and ultrafresh, but not so far out as to risk looking ludicrous ... If the alien planet is covered in ice, we can't have the local inhabitants running round in loincloths.'[100] And what if the planet's glaciated surface was freezing and the inhabitants running round in animal furs? That sounds remarkably lIke Sigma Draconis VI, with the Morgs sensibly wearing animal skins for the cold planet surface and the Eymorgs in skimpier clothes for below surface.

---

[97] Solow and Justman, *Inside Star Trek*, pp370, 399.
[98] Unknown, 'Inflation in 1968 and its effect on dollar value'.
[99] Cushman, *These are the Voyages: TOS Season Three*, p197.
[100] Whitfield and Roddenberry, *The Making of Star Trek*, p356.

Roddenberry never lost faith in Theiss, working with him again on *Pretty Maids All in a Row* (1971), *Genesis II* (1973) and *Planet Earth* (1974), the latter two giving him the opportunity to revisit exotic female costumes. He also developed a spandex bodysuit for *Planet Earth*'s Dylan Hunt, aesthetically only one step away from the uniforms he'd design for **TNG**, his final project with Roddenberry. It was this show for which he'd win the 1988 Emmy for 'Outstanding Achievement in Costuming for a Series'[101] for the episode *The Long Goodbye* (1988).

It's regrettable that with so many fine examples of alien costumes in Bill Theiss' **Star Trek** portfolio, our impression of the Eymorg costume is a design lacking in imagination and execution, and steeped in negative sexual connotations. And how ironic that for a man best remembered for his futuristic, revealing sci-fi female costumes, his only **Star Trek** Emmy was for designs in a 1940s-set holodeck episode.

---

[101] Unknown, 'William Ware Theiss: Awards and Nominations'.

CHAPTER 4. OF MATRIARCHIES, CASUAL SEXISM AND KIRK'S GAZE

Matriarchies

A frequent complaint thrown at *Spock's Brain* is its re-use of the already well-worn science fiction cliché of the matriarchal society. Where **TOS** was ostensibly selling itself as progressive and innovative, here it depended on an overbaked, over-familiar cliché; a retrograde step for the show's storytelling, particularly as the **TOS** iteration would have nothing new to say on the matter.

The heyday of matriarchal science fiction was in the Atomic Age of the 1950s, which saw a proliferation of low budget movies based around the concept – *Abbott and Costello Go to Mars* (1953), *Cat Women of the Moon* (1953), *Fire Maidens from Outer Space* (1956), *Love Slaves of the Amazons* (1957) and *Queen of Outer Space* (1958), among others.

One of the problems with the societies depicted in this genre is that they are almost always inherently unbelievable, both in the way that they came into being and the manner in which they have survived up to that point. In many cases they are flawed ecosystems, ripe for men to challenge.

The Eymorg society is one such problematic matriarchy, and because so little time is spent on explaining how and why the occupants of Sigma Draconis have reached this stage in their evolution, we neither understand nor care about their problems.

At the end of the episode, a newly-revived Spock presents his analysis in a particularly rapid info dump:

> 'A remarkable example of a retrograde civilisation. At the peak, advanced beyond any of our capabilities and now operating at this primitive level which you saw. And it all began thousands of years ago when a glacial age reoccurred. This underground complex was developed for the women. The men remained above, and a male-female schism took place. A fascinating cultural development of a kind which never...'

We assume that Spock picked up this history lesson while his brain was linked to the Eymorg central control system, but for viewers it's too little, too late. At this stage, they are no more invested in the story's logic than the writer presumably was, distraction from the plot logic having been provided by the glamorous, brain-stealing women in their retro sci-fi outfits.

Another common theme with on-screen matriarchies is that they are typically led by a tyrant[102], and that while the stories portray gender division, they usually have nothing new or credible to say about the battle of the sexes. Instead of showing how a female-led society might actually operate, they present a model of an aggressive, belligerent matriarchy, but with fantasy women play-acting the roles, in a dysfunctional regime that's ripe for toppling.

Was the use of a matriarchy in *Spock's Brain* just the flimsiest of excuses for the show to parade a series of 'space babes' in provocative clothing, with the hope of satisfying male viewers with the set dressing of objectified fantasy women? And because they spend most of the hour playing it dumb, they're never seen as a real

---

[102] Examples are looked at later in this chapter.

threat, with even their pain belts being ridiculously easy to remove.

At a time when America's women were trying to claim their rights as second-wave feminism was gaining traction, one reading of the late 60s/early 70s matriarchically-themed fantasy is as a cynical warning from the patriarchy – a cautionary tale – of what might happen if things went too far. Feminism was counterculture and these stories were the establishment's warning to be careful what you wish for, because the outcome might be something even worse than the current imperfect and gender-skewed situation. In the Gene Roddenberry-written **Planet Earth**, lead character Dylan Hunt is captured by women who rule their society by drugging men and keeping them as sex slaves. 'Women's lib, or women's lib gone mad?' he asks[103]. A speculative 'what if' fantasy premise may have been more palatable than a stark, finger-pointing warning that given power, militant feminists could develop into female versions of the tyrants that have been the scourge of our history.

Matriarchal movies

Movies with matriarchal societies were typically set on a distant planet or in the far-flung future, the prospect of such a world being far removed form modern reality. Gene Roddenberry's **Planet Earth** (1973) would rely on a third world war to trigger its change in society, but most of the movies were predisposed to our male heroes leaving the Earth's atmosphere. In *Abbott and Costello Go to Mars* (1953), a rocket ship goes to Venus (they were aiming for Mars!)) where the evil Queen Allura runs a female-led society, men having been long since banished. In a rare deviation from the norm, workmen Lester and Orville don't overthrow the matriarchy, they just come home.

---

[103] See chapter 6.

Venus is a frequent location for these films, the female connection with the Roman goddess of love and beauty being an obvious and useful link, and in *Queen of Outer Space* (1958) Venusian monarch Queen Yllana has killed most men, keeping only mathematicians and scientists alive. This is a society ripe to be overthrown, the women longing to love men again. *Cat-Women of the Moon* (1953) features a female society led by the unitard-wearing Alpha, their lunar atmosphere being depleted and the residents needing to take desperate measures. In a novel variation on the theme, they use mind control on the only female member of the crew to lead the lunar expedition to their base, with plans to steal the rocket ship, return to Earth and: '...get their women under our power, and soon we will rule the whole world!' Fortunately for mankind, cat-woman Lambda has fallen in love with a crew member, thus proving that all they really needed was a good man's affection – she reveals the plot, which is then foiled.

Back on Venus, a team of astronauts discover a colony of women and a single male in *Fire Maidens from Outer Space* (1956), their leader Duessa planning to use the men as mates, as well as to destroy a creature that has been terrorising them. The creature expedites matters by breaking into their city and killing her, before then being killed by the men. Problem solved.

A subgenre of this subgenre is the Amazonian woman society, perhaps best typified by *Love Slaves of the Amazons* (1957). Rather than having to travel to outer space to meet a gang of man-hungry (or man-hating) women, there are unexplored areas of our jungles where such societies exist. In this example, the statuesque green-hued Hulk-like women capture explorers who discover them in the jungles of Brazil and plan to use them as their mates. This plot is mercilessly parodied in **Futurama**'s (1999-2013) Primetime Emmy-nominated episode *Amazon Women in the Mood* (2001).

Sometimes the matriarchies are benign, as in *Nude on the Moon* (1961) where two scientists fly to the Moon (a barely disguised Coral Castle, Florida) and discover a society of topless women led by a caped, telepathic Moon Queen (Marietta), who lets them take photos before they return home. This 'nudie-cutie' features 'moon dolls' in shiny shorts, wearing antennae headbands, and controlling the men via magic wand devices.

In the same month as *Spock's Brain*'s initial transmission, September 1968, director Stanley Kubrick was interviewed about his movie *2001: A Space Odyssey* and said he believed that aliens coming to Earth would likely be benevolent. 'It's hard to think of any other intention that would justify the long and arduous journey from another star,' he suggested. As to the stereotypical depiction of '...bug-eyed monsters, scuttling hungrily after curvaceous Earth maidens,' he clarified:

> 'This probably dates back to the pulp science-fiction magazines of the Twenties and Thirties ... You could have psychotic civilisations or decadent civilisations that have elevated pain to an aesthetic and might covet humans as gladiators or torture objects... or slaves or even for food. While I am appreciably more optimistic, we just can't be sure what their motivations will be.' [104]

In Kubrick's eyes, maybe the Eymorgs with their male slaves and pain/torture devices were not as fanciful as might have been

---

[104] Norden, Eric, 'Playboy Interview: Stanley Kubrick', *Playboy*, Vol. 15, No. 9, September 1968.

thought.

By its 1968 transmission, then, *Spock's Brain* was saying nothing new with its recycling of these well-worn ideas, and yet it wasn't the final word on the subject. Sex comedy *Zeta One* (1969) concerned covert agents led by Zeta from the all-female planet Angvia, infiltrating Earth's ranks of secret agents, while British TV series **Star Maidens** (1976) featured a battle of the sexes courtesy of a female-dominant Medusan society versus the patriarchy of Earth, with both sides coming to a better understanding of the other by the conclusion[105].

Other **Star Trek** series would revisit the matriarchy theme. In **TAS** episode *The Lorelei Signal* (1973), a female society lure men to their planet though siren song and drain them of their life force, a plot line replicated in **Voyager**'s *Favorite Son* (1997), where siren song is substituted with a lure to return men to their alleged place of birth before sucking them dry. And surely Janeway's Queen Arachnia in **Voyager**'s *Bride of Chaotica!* (1999) is modelled on the sort of female tyrants that led matriarchies in the movies we've already covered in detail in this chapter, while also being a throwback to Republic's 1930s serials.

A common theme, and playing to the male fantasy, is that these societies are ripe for male intervention (or interference), even if they don't want it. In *Spock's Brain*, Kirk forces the Eymorgs to give up their ecosystem to go and live on the planet's hostile surface,

---

[105] If you're surprised that **Doctor Who** (1963-) never plundered this story theme for one of its serials, two abandoned stories featured this scenario – 1964's 'The Hidden Planet' and 1968's 'Prison in Space', the latter concerning a society under the control of the malevolent Chairman Babs and her World Federation of Womanhood.

rationalising that they'll be alright. This is a simple, blunt resolution, which is neat and tidy from a TV scripting perspective, but doesn't look into the possibility of helping develop an alternate, sustainable, computerised brain substitute, as happens in the *Story Outline*[106]. Instead, Kirk condemns the current set-up as broken, and lets it collapse by pulling the plug. As with so many of these arrogant male-led expeditions, he wants to make his mark on female society by taming the women or punishing them for non-conforming by putting them back in their place. With his belief that these misguided women were waiting for men to fix their problems, he takes a sledgehammer to crack a walnut.

Arguably, while the current system relies on the theft of an unwilling victim's brain, it **does** actually work. It's morally bankrupt, but it's functioned well for thousands of years, and there's no suggestion it wouldn't continue this way, particularly under the new stewardship of Spock's superior organ. But Kirk wants his science officer back, and risks killing Spock and destroying the planet's life-support system to do so.

The Eymorgs were not waiting for a man to save them – their system was already working efficiently. It's the Morgs who were waiting for their fellow men to rescue them. By the end of the episode, the Morgs were reunited with the female Fymorgs on an equal footing thanks to the intervention of Kirk and his crew. Maybe the Eymorgs will ultimately haver a better life in co-habitation, having been saved by Starfleet? They just didn't know it at the time. This damsel in distress stereotype had already (literally) been demonstrated in *Shore Leave* where Yeoman Burrows revealed her fantasy to be a

---

[106] 11 March 1968, p9.

princess, and was rescued by a knight on a steed.

Writer David Gerrold suggested why he believed this stereotype was perpetuated in **TOS**. 'The need for a heroine in every story is a leftover convention from the era of romanticism... it reduces women to objects. The subliminal message is that a woman is merely a reward for a job well done. Superimposed on a science fiction series – especially **Star Trek** is unreal. No, it's surreal.' [107]

One way to read *Spock's Brain* is that the Eymorgs are a race of women needing assistance from a man to make their society work. That assistance is in the form of a male brain, or Kirk's actions that force them into a new way of living on the planet's surface. In the episode's *Story Outline*[108] the mixed gender race that the *Enterprise* crew meet are not Eymorgs/Morgs but the Nefelese, and they explain why they researched and deliberately sought Spock's brain to power their civilisation. In the televised version, we have no idea why the Vulcan science officer was the Eymorg's target. Did the Teacher give them this insight, having shortlisted the best candidates for the role? And must the brain be male? It could have been a very different story if the Eymorgs had opted for a female brain to replace their current organ, though that would have limited the potential abductees from the *Enterprise* to Uhura, Chapel or the yeoman of the week. It's because Spock's male brain is chosen that the female dominance is immediately undermined – everything they say and do will be controlled by a man.

When describing a typical **TOS** 'formula' story, David Gerrold created a potential scenario. 'Kirk, Spock and McCoy get captured by six-foot

---

[107] Gerrold, *The World of Star Trek*, p227.
[108] 11 March 1968, p7. See chapter 5.

green women in steel brassieres. They take away the spacemen's communicators because they offend the computer-gods that these women worship.' He continued, referring to the crew working against a countdown and being kept in a dungeon: 'the seduced priestess promises Kirk that she will work to build a new civilisation on her planet – just for Kirk – one where women's lib and steel brassieres will be illegal.'[109] Does that summary sound remarkably familiar?

In an essay on sexism in **Star Trek**, Mary Jo Deegan summarises that

> 'In every romantic episode, human women are introduced either as evil temptresses or as culturally and morally superior but sexually unavailable temptresses. Yet they can be legitimately attractive. Female aliens, however, are usually just stupid and vicious, and provide opportunities for the extreme depiction of females as limited and despicable beings.'[110]

It's a harsh insight, but perfectly encapsulates the sexist, negative qualities of the Eymorgs – stupid ('Brain and Brain. What is Brain?') and vicious ('They are givers of pain and delight').

Throughout *Spock's Brain*, the Eymorgs are judged to be naïve and simple – McCoy says of them: 'Jim, it's no use... you'll get nothing out of that one. Hers is the mind of a child.' He continues 'Her mind is functioning on a very simple level. Her faculties are atrophied because of non-use.' Later Kirk asks 'How is this place kept functioning by the primitive minds we've met?'

---

[109] Gerrold, *The World of Star Trek*, p233.
[110] Deegan, Mary Jo, 'Sexism in Space: The Freudian Formula in Star Trek' in Palumbo, Donald, ed, *Eros in the Mind's Eye: Sexuality and the Fantastic in Art and Film*, p215.

With their childlike intellect and arrested development there's the opportunity to casually perpetuate the stereotype of the 'dumb woman' or the 'airhead'. This ditzy female has been the source of much sexist humour – Goldie Hawn played this persona as one of her characters in **Rowan and Martin's Laugh-In** (1968-1973), a popular comedy show at the time of *Spock's Brain*'s transmission, and the show that would 'steal' **TOS** Series 3's promised Monday time slot.

The landing party cannot understand how the women they meet were able to develop the technology that runs the planet, as well as creating ships with advanced ion drives, let alone have the knowledge to perform brain surgery. They don't believe it because the women do not have the IQs or mental capacity to do so – McCoy's tricorder has said as much, though just how does a machine measure this? Is it based on an analysis of vocabulary, of IQ, their life experience? What's the baseline? Even a child knows what a brain is. But a conditioned, sexist mind in 1968 might also be subliminally thinking: 'they couldn't have achieved any of this, because they are women – dumb women at that – and women aren't suited to engineering.' Scott insists 'Those women could never have set up anything as complex as this has to be. Why, that takes engineering genius. But there's no sign of engineering genius in any of those women.' It was an opinion that existed outside of the fantasy world of **TOS**. As NASA legend Katherine Johnson demonstrated (as popularised in the movie *Hidden Figures* (2016)) it was a battle to prove that a woman could be accepted as a proficient, credible scientist. It's sobering to think that in response to the Soviet Union launching female cosmonaut Valentina Tereshkova into space in the summer of 1963, astronaut John Glenn said '...so far we felt the qualifications we were looking for... we're best taken care of by men.'

And that an unidentified NASA spokesman was even directly quoted as saying that talk of an American space woman 'makes me sick at my stomach.'[111]

Following the crew's logic, because the women are infantile, they are also gullible. Kirk flatters them and throws himself down on his knees. 'Great leader. Great leader! We come from a far place to learn from your Controller.'[112] Later, Kara, even when recently powered-up from a session with the Teacher, is tricked by Mr Scott's elementary diversion so that Kirk can steal his phaser back from her.

By being infantilised, the women are subjected to another form of sexism. Unless they've been injected by a dose of the male Teacher's knowledge, these females are 'girls', subject to the negative connotations that come with that. They are identified as targets to be patronised; being labelled as child or girl strips away a woman's adult attributes and the power that comes with adulthood. In the same way that a child is typically subservient to a parent, Kirk assumes a paternal role, talking down to the Eymorg girls, assuming a position of superiority courtesy of his adult, male status. Even the Eymorg pain device control looks like a child's toy, comprising simple buttons, though McCoy's remote-control device for Spock is little better in its aesthetic design.

And because he has the gender and intellectual high ground over the child-like Eymorgs, this being a classic example of Kirk taking the opportunity to 'mansplain' why his solution is for the best.

---

[111] Luce, Clare Booth, 'Some People Simply Never Get the Message', *Time*, Vol 54, No.26, 28 June 1963.
[112] Incidentally, Kara is not taken in by Kirk's dramatic antics here.

> KARA
>
> We will die above in the cold.
>
> KIRK
>
> No, you won't. You'll learn to build houses, to keep warm, to work. We'll help you for a while. Humans have survived under worse conditions. It's a matter of evolution. You'll be fine.

'You'll be fine.' It's a non-scientific way for Kirk to shut down an argument and justify his extreme resolution. He has broken the infrastructure that a highly advanced community of women has been running for thousands of years and now considers he's in a position to tell them how best to run their world. And it most certainly is not a matter of evolution.

It's the sort of patronising behaviour seen elsewhere in *The Lights of Zetar* (1969) when Scott talks to his new colleague (and blossoming love interest) Mira on her first deep space trip. She collapses and starts talking in a slow, alien language, but he puts this down to her getting her space legs. When her answers to questions from McCoy don't add up, Scott intervenes paternalistically. 'She just didn't understand. Did you now, lass?' Kirk continues 'Is the girl well enough to be questioned?' *Lass, girl* – it's the use of patronising gender-specific language to assume control of a conversation. When working out what happened to Spock's brain, Kirk exclaims: 'That girl!' He's referring to the mysterious woman that appeared on his ship, and who momentarily mesmerised those who saw her. But in his eyes, a female adult who has potentially stolen a brain is just 'that girl'.

Objectification

While the treatment of the Eymorgs as unintelligent children is cause enough for concern, their sexualisation through objectification must also be highlighted. Objectification is the act of treating a person as an object, the victim being stripped of their human qualities, instead being identified by how their body looks. This might include taking away their voice or speech, something that happens to the Eymorgs when they are presented in their more primitive state. While not mute, they are presented as such simple creatures that the crew cannot engage with them in meaningful conversation, and the eye is instead diverted to their appearance.

One key arena for female objectification is heterosexual pornography, its female participants typically reduced to dehumanised objects of desire, dressed in sexualised clothing. The narratives (flimsy as they are) can contain elements of those involved receiving or giving pleasure or pain.

The **Sex Trek** adult movie series used **TOS** plotlines as the inspiration for its low budget porn parodies, with *Spock's Brain* the basis for *Space Trek II: The Search for Sperm* (1991). The crew of the USS *Plunderer* are rendered in stasis when an alien woman beams onto the ship. When they recover, Mr Sperm is found unconscious in sickbay, with his penis removed. His brain is also missing, because In his species the brain is contained in the genitals. The crew follow an ionised trail to the planet Thewomb, which is inhabited solely by women, where the landing party is overcome by the thief, who attaches obedience collars to them. They release themselves by gaining access to the control bracelet and Doctor McJoy reattaches Mr Sperm's penis.

Writer Cash Markman confirmed why this story was an obvious choice for parody.

> '*Spock's Brain* had a great deal of male fantasies at play... I didn't have to stray far from the source material to make a campy sex romp. ... Another reason I chose *Spock's Brain* was that it had a mini-skirted, go-go-booted dominatrix in the episode."

In addition to having the story elements that fit the needs of an adult film, the episode was chosen for another, more practical reason.

> 'I knew this outfit that hired me wasn't up to doing a very good job.... So, I felt it was best if they were given a truly inane story to shoot. And what could be more inane than a really bad parody of a really bad episode.'[113]

The 'brain as penis' or 'penis as brain' idea is pursued more seriously in Mary Jo Deegan's assessment of *Spock's Brain*.

> 'In one of **Star Trek**'s most complicated deprecations of women, yet another priestess steals Spock's brain and installs it in the computer that empowers her to act and requires the brain to continue functioning...This story of a computer-controlled woman stealing a man's brain is an intricate seduction/castration fantasy that dramatizes the evil power of mindless women.'[114]

And if the removal of the brain could represent the removal of the penis, the words were seen as interchangeable in the *#SpocksDick* series of Tweets. In October 2017, Twitter user @swear_trek

---

[113] Author interview, 4 May 2021.
[114] Deegan, 'Sexism in Space', p216.

released 21 silent clips of between 10 and 50 seconds from *Spock's Brain* with spoken dialogue replaced with subtitles. The only difference to the original script was that every use of the word 'brain' was replaced by the word 'dick'. The hashtag #spocksdick trended, with over 115,000 views of the first instalment. It may have been puerile, but it resonated with thousands of social media users and reaffirmed that the episode is seen as fair game for mockery.

Kirk's Gaze

Objectification is typically seen through the male viewpoint, often referred to as the male gaze. This filtered view of a woman strips away all but their beauty and sexuality. In **TOS**, it's typically Kirk's gaze, as he's our lead.

When we see Kara and her fellow Eymorgs, the camera draws us to (and lingers on) their looks: their beauty, the clothing that accentuates their legs and the glimpses of flesh on the thighs and under the halterneck. McCoy sniggers 'I'm sure you noticed the delight aspect of this place.' It has not gone unnoticed. Herb Solow later confirmed that:

> 'Yes, actresses were chosen for their acting talent, but voluptuous lips and seductive eyes were very important to him [Gene Roddenberry]. And in most instances, the characters they portrayed were emotionally subordinate to the men of **Star Trek**. Women were, essentially, sex objects always ready for action.'[115]

Betty Friedan observed of women on TV in 1964: 'Even when the face and body of a woman are there, one feels a strange vagueness and

---

[115] Solow and Justman, *Inside Star Trek*, p226.

emptiness, an absence of human identity.' These hollow, detached women are a mishmash of obsolete prejudices where a: '...woman is inferior, child-like, animal-like, incapable of thought or action or contribution to society.' [116]

A fairly comprehensive description of the Eymorgs in 1968, showing how little had changed in four years.

There are many examples of sexist comments in **TOS** where the female is casually the butt of a joke or an unproven myth. When Nomad is scanning crew members on the *Enterprise* bridge in *The Changeling* (1967), it stops to read Lieutenant Uhura. 'That unit is defective. Its thinking is chaotic. Absorbing it unsettled me,' it reports to Spock. Leaving just enough time to hit a comedy beat, the Vulcan science officer replies with 'That unit is a woman,' and Nomad adds to the sexism with: 'A mass of conflicting impulses.' It's disappointing that the highly-intelligent Spock would be given such an unscientific comment, regardless of its sexism.

Equally bewildering is his explanation why women are being targeted by an unknown killer on Argelius in *Wolf in the Fold* (1967). Kirk deduces that the creature feeds on horror and fear, assuming a physical shape to kill, to which Spock adds: 'And I suspect preys on women because women are more easily and more deeply terrified, generating more sheer horror than the male of the species.' If it wasn't bad enough that the women of this pleasure planet were depicted as freely available sex objects in a hedonistic society, the science is also lousy.

Is it the sexism or bad science that's more embarrassing in this

---

[116] Friedan, 'Television and the Female Mystique', p93.

episode, which had already depicted the women of this pleasure planet as freely available sex objects in a hedonistic society?

If *Wolf in the Fold* reveals a failed cure for misogyny, the female-hating trait is even more centre stage in the show's final episode, the Gene Roddenberry-written *Turnabout Intruder*. Kirk's former flame Janice Lester switches bodies with the captain but is unable to maintain the illusion that she's Kirk because of her displays of 'emotional instability and erratic mental attitudes' and 'Her intense hatred of her own womanhood [which] made life with her impossible.' She is bitter that the: world of starship captains doesn't admit women', Lester is presented as a bitter, scheming, hateful woman who would happily see Kirk blamed for her own actions. She loses her career, but her greatest regret is that Kirk will 'never know the indignity of being a woman... believe me it's better to be dead than alone in the body of a woman.' The greater shame is 'Her life could have been as rich as any woman's. If only. If only.' It's an angry, misogynistic portrait of woman that showcases some of the worst excesses of female-kind.

Feminist Gail Collins even mentions this episode in her bestselling book *When Everything Changed*:

> 'the original **Star Trek** series would feature a story about a woman so desperate to become a starship captain – a post apparently restricted to men – that she arranged to have her brain transferred into Captain Kirk's body. The crew quickly noticed that the captain was manicuring his nails at the helm and having hysterics over the least little thing.'[117]

---

[117] Collins, *When Everything Changed*, p14.

As an example of casual sexism, Spock and Kirk's conversation in *Elaan of Troyius* (1968) is notable.

SPOCK

Captain, your analysis of the situation was flawless, anticipating that she would deny you admittance. However, the logic by which you arrived at your conclusion escapes me.

KIRK

Mister Spock, the women on your planet are logical. That's the only planet in this galaxy that can make that claim.

Aggression and sexual violence

Another sexist theme in *Spock's Brain* is its use of aggression and violence towards women. After McCoy tells Kirk that he didn't have the ability to replace Spock's brain, Kirk threatens 'The thief that took it has the knowledge. I'll force it out of her.' When he encounters Luma in the Eymorg bunker, Kirk initially stuns her, and after McCoy has revived her, she's dragged to her feet, held forcibly about the upper arms, shaking her and grabbing her tighter. When she pleads ignorance Kirk accuses her of lying and then, in what could be seen as a sinister threat, insists he has no wish to hurt her.

When he meets Kara, she chides him for his aggression: 'You hurt Luma. It is not permitted again to hurt anyone.' His apology doesn't convince. 'Sorry. We don't want to hurt anyone.' Spock is later directed by Kirk to restrain Kara and holds her by the wrists. Kirk takes over, shaking her: 'Now, you took his brain. You will put it back. How did you do it?' When the Teacher helmet is identified as an interface with the main control system, Spock informs Kirk: 'Its use is strictly predetermined by the builders.' But he ignores both this warning and the pleas from Kara, pulling down the transparent helmet over her head and creating a connection. At this time, he has no idea of how the technology works – it might wipe her mind or kill her, and yet he recklessly presses ahead, hoping that he made the right decision.

Kara survives the download of information and draws a phaser on Kirk – an exaggerated yawn from Mr Scott gives him the diversion to disarm her. The last action is probably the least objectionable of Kirk's otherwise aggressive series of negotiations with the Eymorgs. While we give him the benefit of the doubt that he is probably emotional because he's running out of time in which to save his first officer, he's still a leader, a representative of Starfleet, and this shouldn't extend to thinly-veiled threats of torture and the subsequent brutal action of forcing Teacher onto Kara's head without her consent

Spock's Brain was not the only instance where violence towards women was threatened or carried out in **TOS**. In *Friday's Child* (1967) McCoy is scanning Capellan dignitary Eleen and places his hand on her belly. She objects: 'You will not touch me in that manner.' Rather than respecting cultural difference or a woman's right to decide how her own body is treated, he responds 'I'll touch you in any way or manner that my professional judgment indicates'. She slaps his face twice... and astonishingly he feels entitled to slap her back! From slaps to spanking, Kirk threatens the haughty queen in *Elaan of Troyius* (1968): 'If I touch you again, Your Glory, it'll be to administer an ancient Earth custom called a spanking. A form of punishment administered to spoilt brats.' Within minutes they're kissing and she asks provocatively 'Captain, that ancient Earth custom called spanking, what is it?'

Female violence may here be the subject of an ill-judged joke, but it's nowhere near as ill-judged as the concluding moment of *The Enemy Within*. In this episode, Kirk is split into two bodies – one good, one evil – the evil one roaming the ship with a bottle of Saurian brandy as the other remains in sickbay. Evil Kirk visits Yeoman Rand in her quarters. 'You're too beautiful to ignore. Too much woman. We've both been pretending too long', he professes, before grabbing her. 'Stop pretending. Let's stop pretending. Come here, Janice. Don't fight me. Don't fight me, Janice.' He kisses her before forcing her onto the floor and sexually assaulting her. She escapes by scratching his face, reaching the door and catching the attention of a passing guard. She asks him to alert Spock, who believes her story and comes to the conclusion that there's an imposter on board. It's a shocking moment, and yet its integrity is undermined by making it the subject of a joke. Spock is on the bridge, raises an eyebrow and asks Rand: 'The imposter had some interesting qualities, wouldn't you say, yeoman?' Interesting how? Did trying to rape her make him interesting?

Grace Lee Whitney condemned the moment as: '...a badly botched attempt at humour... I can't imagine any more cruel and insensitive a comment a man (or Vulcan) could make to a woman who had just gone through a sexual assault.... [the writer] gives us a leering Mr Spock who suggests that Yeoman Rand **enjoyed** being raped...'[118]

It's disappointing that many of the viewers who watched the episode at the time of transmission or subsequently would have suffered their own experiences of sexual assault, and the optimistic, futuristic world of **TOS** was confirming that even 300 years in the future, such

---

[118] Whitney, *The Longest Trek*, p95.

behaviour would be treated as a joke. In a cruel case of life imitating art, a few weeks after filming, Grace Lee Whitney alleges that she was the victim of real-life sexual assault by a studio executive.[119]

As seen on TV

Before concluding this assessment of the themes in *Spock's Brain*, there's value in being familiar with other content that was being shown on US network TV and at US cinemas around the late September 1968 original transmission. Providing this context helps measure whether the episode was in line with contemporary media, behind the times, or leading the way.

Across the television networks, female-led shows and those with strong female leads would continue to be shown. On NBC, sit-com **Julia** (1968-71) began a three-season run, starring Diahann Carroll as Julia Baker, a recently widowed black nurse. It was lauded for being the first situation comedy to feature an African American in a non-stereotypical role; in the opening episode, widow Julia applies for a job at an aerospace company.

Lucille Ball (former CEO of **TOS**'s production company Desilu) returned to TV in comedy **Here's Lucy** (1968-74), following Lucy Carter, a widowed mother with a son and daughter, working as a secretary at an LA employment agency. Other female-centric shows were returnees **The Mothers-in-Law** (1967-69) and vehicles for comedians – **The Beautiful Phyllis Diller Show**[120] (1968), **The Carol Burnett Show** (1967-78) and **The Doris Day Show** (1968-73). The widow theme continued with the TV remake of 1947 movie **The**

---

[119] Whitney, *The Longest Trek*, p95.
[120] A curiously sexist title for a female-hosted show.

Ghost and Mrs Muir (1968-70) with Hope Lange as a widowed writer bringing up her children while haunted by chauvinistic ghost Captain Gregg, as well as in **Petticoat Junction** (1963-70), a comedy about a hotel run by widow Kate Bradley, her uncle and three daughters

On ABC, **The Mod Squad** (1968-73) trio of undercover cops included Peggy Lipton as no-nonsense 'it girl' Julie Barnes, while in **Get Smart** (1965-70) Barbara Feldon's Agent 99 continued to prove herself as more competent than CONTROL colleague Maxwell Smart. UK import **The Avengers** began its seventh season with the departure of Mrs Peel and the introduction of Linda Thorson's single woman spy Tara King. Barbara Bain returned for her third and final season of **Mission: Impossible** as IMF agent Cinnamon Carter – fashion model, actor and femme fatale. And while she frequently play-acted the damsel in distress, this was typically to gain the confidence of a vain man who would then drop his defences and share his secrets. Barbara Anderson reprised her role as plain clothed police officer Eve Whitfield in **Ironside** (1967-75), her performance garnering her an Emmy this season.

What are these shows telling us about the TV landscape of late 1968? In summary, female-led comedies were regular fixtures of the schedules. Often widows, these strong women were establishing their own careers without relying on men, and typically bringing up children. In dramas, strong female leads were spies or agents, holding their own against (and often being smarter than) their male co-stars and villains of the week. Contrast these entries with *Spock's Brain*, a show whose female regulars played minor supporting roles in the drama, and featuring a society of unintelligent, sexualised women. While this episode could be seen as blip, the **TOS** female regulars had little more to do for the rest of the season, with exception of the occasional away mission – Uhura and Chapel joined left the *Enterprise* in *Plato's Stepchildren* (1969).

And what of the casual sexism revealed in *Spock's Brain*? Was it prevalent elsewhere? A good case study is the season opener of **Bewitched** (1964-72) one of the two main well-established sitcoms with female leads, returning this season for its fifth year.[121]

In **Bewitched**'s *Samantha's Wedding Present* (26 September 1968) domestic witch Samantha (Elizabeth Montgomery) and husband Darrin (Dick York) continue to be plagued by well-meaning but interfering mother-in-law Endora (Agnes Moorhead). She buys Samantha a belated wedding present which incenses Darrin He makes a stand as man of the house and expresses his disapproval. Offended, Endora casts a spell which reduces him to pocket-size because he's 'a small small man'... It's a fun half hour, much of the sexism aimed at Darrin's stubborn bigotry, arrogance and failure to read the situation.

In Samantha we have a strong woman – she wields greater power than her husband and yet is willing to hide her magical powers to maintain stronger than her husband, keeping her magical powers magic hidden away so as not to disturb the status quo. Samantha is living her best life; on the face of it she's the antithesis of the stereotypical woman portrayed on American TV, and as criticised by feminist Betty Friedan, and yet she's still stuck in the kitchen. The author of the bestselling *The Feminine Mystique* (1963) applied her observations to an overview of American TV in a February 1964 *TV Guide* essay. She argued:

---

[121] **I Dream of Jeannie** (1965-70) was the other; the points raised regarding **Bewitched** apply here too.

> 'If the image of women on television today reflects – or affects reality, then American women must be writhing in agonies of self-contempt and unappeasable hunger. Television's image of the American woman, 1964, is a stupid, unattractive, insecure little household drudge who spends her martyred, mindless, boring days dreaming of love – and plotting nasty revenge against her husband.'[122]

Samantha doesn't plot nasty revenge against Darrin, though she frequently delights in him seeing the error of his ways. Friedman summarised it succinctly when she said: 'Evidently, in order to retain her 'femininity', [the] wife always had to lose the battle in the end – or rather demonstrate her true superiority by magnanimously letting the poor fool think he won it.[123]

Of **Bewitched**, science fiction writer Isaac Asimov would write in 1969, in a mock discussion between himself and his more 'enlightened' daughter, that it was 'a monstrous production that is destroying all that is most holy and wonderful in the husband-wife relationship because it is representing a woman who is in control of the situations around her, and a husband who is patently not in control of them.' He continued: 'Here's a woman with unimaginable power, and she uses it to shore up her husband's ego, make him look good, help him keep his job, beat down his enemies. Has she no life of her own?'[124] The style and tone of the article (even the title *Husbands Beware!*) suggest that maybe we shouldn't take Asimov

---

[122] Friedan, 'Television and the Female Mystique', p93.
[123] Friedan, 'Television and the Female Mystique', p95.
[124] Asimov, Isaac, 'Husbands, Beware!' *TV Guide*, March 22-28, 1969, pp7-10.

too seriously here.

If the fall's new TV season was consciously striving towards a better gender mix, so too was the US movie output. *Funny Girl* (1968) was the year's top-grossing movie, an Oscar-winning performance from Barbra Streisand as comedian and singer Fanny Brice, released the day before *Spock's Brain*. With strong support from Ann Francis and Kay Medford, the movie's popularity demonstrated the appreciation of a female-led vehicle, one which was not scared to address Brice's battle in not being the typical classic beauty. And yet for all of *Funny Girl*'s positive depiction of women, *Playboy* for September 1968 boasted a 10-page 'Pictorial preview of the cinematic lovelies who beautify the upcoming Barbra Streisand musical,' showcasing female actors from the movie in topless shots.

If *Funny Girl* was the calling card for the modern feminist, *Barbarella* (1968), on the surface at least, feels less enlightened. Released three weeks after *Spock's Brain*, Barbarella features Jane Fonda's eponymous 41st century explorer. Directed by Roger Vadim – who would later helm Gene Roddenberry's *Pretty Maids All in a Row* (1973) – the movie features Barbarella in a series of retro-futuristic fetishist costumes that would not be out of place on the Eymorgs. Barbarella is a male fantasy, but unlike the denizens of Sigma Draconis VI, she doesn't need a man to give her agency. She owns her sexuality and is no less intelligent than any of the other characters in the movie – we're told that she's a five-star, double-rated Astro-navigatrix. She's constantly objectivised – the opening scene is her stripping out of a spacesuit in zero gravity – but she also takes the lead in sex as it suits her. At one point she agrees to make love with Mark Hand rather than using the exaltation transference pellets (sex pills) she's been using, and by sleeping with Jon Philp

Law's blind angel Pygar she awakens his ability to fly.

Anita Pallenberg is villain the Great Tyrant, her vicious queen a throwback to 1940s pulp novels, as indeed are many of the movie's aspects. Sporting a unicorn horn on her head at one point, she cries in horror when Barbarella threatens to melt her face with a ray gun: 'My face, my beautiful face. How dare you threaten my face!' she screams with stereotypical feminine vanity. Another similarity with *Spock's Brain* is Durand-Durand's 'excessive pleasure machine', a contraption that induces fatal sexual pleasure, sharing the 'givers of pleasure and pain' modus operandi of the Eymorgs' pain belts. Barbarella has the staying power to survive the planned death by orgasm and blows the instrument's fuses, concluding a movie that mocks prudish approaches to morality and emphasising the single woman's empowerment to live her life as she pleases, while presenting her as a desirable sex object for heterosexual males.

From *Barbarella* to Barbara, Judith O'Dea's character in *The Night of the Living Dead* (1968) merits a mention. As main protagonist of the first instalment of George A Romero's zombie series, released on the first of October, she's a strong female lead, fighting off zombies while trapped in a farmhouse. Instead of the screaming victim waiting to be rescued, Barbara takes control when her brother is attacked by a zombie at their parents' graveside.

In his write-up of *Spock's Brain* for the 25 September 1968 edition of *Weekly Variety*, reviewer Mor complained that while the chief characters were largely caricatures delivering turgid dialogue: '...for males of all ages at least, it also retains a bevy of shapely femmes in tight and revealing space suits...'[125] The message seems to be that if

---

[125] Cushman, *These are the Voyages: TOS Season Three*, p200.

character and dialogue fall by the wayside, you can at least take solace in titivation.

CHAPTER 5: VERSION CONTROL
What Went Wrong?

For anyone with an interest in television production, hearing that the final televised version is considerably different to what was originally written in the first outline, is unlikely to generate a Spock-like raise of the eyebrows. Change is par for the course with TV, as producers and other interested parties make changes for creative, financial, practical and countless other reasons. But in the case of *Spock's Brain*, the changes were so great that if the televised version had been more like Coon's initial vision, I believe that the episode would not be at the sharp end of our analysis, and certainly not be criticised for its poor depiction of women.

One of the bitterest pills to swallow about *Spock's Brain* is that it's written by Gene L Coon, albeit under the pseudonym of Lee Cronin. This is the man who served as **TOS**' producer from Season 1's *Miri* to Season 2's *A Private Little War*, who created the Klingons in *Errand of Mercy* (1967) and added Khan to *Space Seed*, while also rewriting drafts of other writers' work. This impressive back catalogue suggests a professional who knew how to write a good script, so what went wrong with *Spock's Brain*?

By following the development of Coon's *Spock's Brain* from outline to final televised version, we notice significant changes happening along the way, introduced by producer, executive producer and director. Few were to the benefit of the show, and the sexist nature of the episode barely exists at the outset. Analysis of these documents will show how a mixed society of diminutive aliens became a matriarchy of statuesque space maidens and how the involvement of others changed it from being a straight script to a semi-comedy.

Originally brought in as line producer to replace departing John D F Black – he was fourth choice after Fred Freiberger, Samuel A Peeples and James Goldstone all declined[126] – Coon immediately impressed his bosses. Said Associate Producer Robert Justman '...I've never seen anyone before who could, when a script needed to be written, sit down in two days and not only knock out a script, but the script would be 20 or 30 pages too long[127].' He continues 'Although his title was "Producer", Coon knew he was hired to write, and write he did. He was an ever-fertile source of story ideas and "the fastest typewriter in the West." Coon churned out page after page of shootable and exciting scripts...'[128] Quality and quantity were in abundance from a producer, who was 'fresh and strong and oblivious to pressure, [and] became **Star Trek**'s saviour and Justman's new "hero."'[129]

But by Season 3, Coon would have other priorities. Having now left the show, Coon had an exclusivity contract at Universal where he was writing for Robert Wagner crime-caper **It Takes a Thief** (1968-70). His extra-curricular work on **TOS** was moonlighting, and the quality of his script suggests someone under pressure, or with limited time to spend on crafting and redrafting. Maybe he didn't have the time to challenge the suggested changes, and now being a writer for hire, he didn't have the clout of a producer.

Of his story pitches for Season 3, four were commissioned, becoming

---

[126] Cushman, *These are the Voyages: TOS Season One*, p280.
[127] Solow and Justman, *Inside Star Trek*, p33.
[128] Solow and Justman, *Inside Star Trek*, p206.
[129] Solow and Justman, *Inside Star Trek*, p205.

Spock's Brain, *Spectre of the Gun* (1968), *Wink of an Eye* (1968) and *Let That Be Your Last Battlefield* (1969). While he would complete multiple draft scripts for the first two, he was released from screenwriting duties for *Wink* and *Battlefield* because of his time constraints, and would receive 'Story by' credits in the final episodes, their teleplays being respectively written by Arthur Heinemann and Oliver Crawford.

It's important to restate Coon's credentials, summarising what he'd already achieved on **TOS** before writing *Spock's Br*ain, because it makes the likelihood of him turning in a poor, sexist script less likely. It's possible that he had less fight or influence to challenge the changes that were being suggested on a show that was managing the loss of key personnel (Gene Roddenberry and D C Fontana) and trying to produce a weekly episode with a new producer and a new budget of $178,500[130] per episode (a drop of $9,000 on the previous year's budget, not taking into account inflation and increased wages for the main cast). **TOS** writer David Gerrold says that Coon described **TOS** as '...the hardest show in television history to write for'[131]. Looking at the story of *Spock's Brain*, the writing was just part of the challenge. Of Coon's writing on this episode, Roddenberry would observe in his memo of 10 July 1968 to producer Fred Freiberger: 'I certainly appreciate the hard work and incredible speed... It is not surprising the speed would result in certain problem areas.'[132] The cracks were starting to show

---

[130] Solow and Justman, *Inside Star Trek*, p399.
[131] Gerrold, *The World of Star Trek*, p177.
[132] Cushman, *These are the Voyages: TOS Season Three*, p187.

Story Outline: March 11, 1968

The 10-page typed outline begins with a teaser of Spock exploring a small asteroid, where he's separated from Kirk and McCoy. When later found in a cave by his crewmates, McCoy pronounces Spock dead and that his brain has been removed. He's returned to the *Enterprise* where his body is 'tied in with body functions mechanisms to keep it alive.' At this stage, Spock's body will be useless after a few days, this being a ticking clock that will vary across versions. Kirk and his crew track down the thief to a 'heavily populated, highly civilised' planet and the captain threatens to use force if they are not allowed to beam down. This is a planet of diminutive people, 'who evidently wouldn't hurt a fly' and are terrified by the threat of violence. The planet, Nefel, is controlled by a complicated life support system and led by male Ehr Von, who is surrounded by 'exquisitely beautiful, tiny women' as well as small men who have not used weapons 'for several millenniums' (sic). When trying to contact the *Enterprise*, Kirk picks up Spock's voice on his communicator – the Vulcan is in a dark void.

On Nefel, the crew are cared for by 'lovely young women, all of whom are most tender and considerate.' Ehr Von confesses that they have taken Spock's brain to run the planet's central control system. Previously, the system was run by an eternal, volunteer brain, which was injured during an accident. Studying from afar, they choose Spock's brain as a suitable replacement. Kirk argues that, unlike the original brain donor, Spock did not volunteer his organ, and asks him to go into the Vulcan state of total, complete mental control – *slon porra*. Systems start shutting down on the planet, and Spock's brain is revealed to be floating in a transparent box of fluid. Surgery is carried out by McCoy, Ehr Von and Nefelese surgeons, giving him hints of 'things he had never even guessed at.' The operation is successful, Spock provides a computer to run the Nefelese system (without the need of an organic brain) and bickers with McCoy about how the surgery resulted in some of his functions being switched – he wants to sneeze, but instead uncharacteristically laughs. Kirk suggests that the next time a culture needs a brain, he'll volunteer both of them for the job and that way they'd all get some peace.

This isn't a matriarchal society; it's run by both males and females. The women are helpful, not domineering, there's no suggestion that one sex is intellectually inferior to the other, or to the visiting humans. The people might be beautiful, but they're diminutive, not statuesque, and there's no description of overly-provocative clothing or practices to control the men. In short, most of the problems raised in earlier chapters with the televised episode are not here.

Script Draft 1: April 16, 1968

It's easy to guess why the following lines from this version of the script would be rewritten in subsequent drafts.

KIRK

A dead and buried city... a planet in a glacial age...

GILLIAM

And a male humanoid who doesn't know the meaning of the word female.

KIRK

Put them together...

MCCOY

And it comes out incomprehensible.

Presumably unintentionally, it highlighted one of the big issues with the story even at this stage... it was indeed playing out as 'incomprehensible.'

We begin on the bridge of the *Enterprise*, the crew monitoring a 'slender, needlelike [sic]' ship. Spock picks up three humanoid readings with a low level of metabolism, suggesting sickness or injury. A rescue attempt results in only one figure being beamed to the Transporter Room. She's referred to in the directions as Mea, and hits a button on her belt to immobilise the crew, before locating Spock. The crew recover after several 'terrestrial hours' and McCoy now has Spock wired up to life support, his brain having been removed, but unlikely to live longer than a week in this condition. New character, Assistant Science Officer, Lieutenant Gilliam, '...a burly black man with the look of an athlete,' assumes Spock's role and helps locate the thief to the Omega Alpha IV system, where Kirk choses which planet to search.

New character, Security Head Alexandrovitch, beams down first to Omega Alpha IV, accompanied by his security team of redshirts – Ito, Corelli and Burns. They're followed by Kirk, Scott, McCoy, Gilliam and Chekov, all sensibly wearing lightweight thermal cold weather gear in anticipation of the glacial environment. Having captured a primitive local, the crew use the universal translator to question him, and he leads them to the entrance to a hidden city. After deliberately triggering a trap, the crew descend to the subterranean chamber where they encounter metal collar-wearing men in leather halters, accompanied by a slight girl, who touches a button on her belt, ringing for help. Kirk uses the universal translator to talk to her.

Their leader is Mea, who stole the brain, and is fully aware of what she did, not denying her actions. They go to Central Control, where they find a life support system and metallic helmet '...which feeds the knowledge of the ancients into the minds of whoever wears the helmet.' Mea puts on the helmet to allow her to better communicate and we witness the intelligence, the knowledge and wisdom flooding into her. With only a universal translator at their disposal, a voice is picked up by the party, describing something as 'illogical'. It doesn't sound like Spock, because all voices sound the same on the universal translator, but it's unquestionably him.

Kirk deduces that the city's systems are running like a life support system, the air coming in and out like a set of lungs, with a brain running it. Something must have happened to the brain they previously had, and they tracked down the best replacement in the galaxy, that of a trained Vulcan. Removing it will destroy the life support system of a world, perhaps the death of millions. Having had their control collars removed, the burly captors help the away party escape. Gilliam observes that the genders are sexually divided: 'the women the most advanced. They snare men when they're needed... and control them...'

Realising that they can no longer control the men, the women cower away in sheer terror. Recognising that the control helmet can transmit specialist knowledge, albeit for a short period of time, Kirk convinces a reluctant McCoy to download the skills to complete brain surgery. The operation is successfully completed by McCoy back on the *Enterprise*, supported by Nurse Chapel. New character Sociology Lieutenant McAdams is tasked with assessing and managing the rejoining of the two sexes on the planet. Spock returns to his duties, criticising McCoy for some functions which got mixed up in the surgery. Spock informs us that his race is propagated by mail. How this would work in a practical sense is not elaborated on.

This version of the story is very different to the original, and a number of the problematic sexist issues have crept in. When Mea appears on the Bridge she's '...an absolutely radiantly beautiful woman, wearing a simple, flowing iridescent short tunic... a great deal of her body showing, and it is quite a body to show...', and when her companions arrive: 'Three more WOMEN appear, all lovely, all wearing the same costume, except for individual trims... for they are women, and not really interested in uniforms.' Women in general aren't interested in uniforms, or just these ones? It's a bizarre claim. But even more concerning is the misogyny in some of the lines of dialogue. When Kirk suggests this is possibly a matter of telepathy or nonverbal communication, Scott replies, rather unscientifically: 'Developed by a bunch of women? Never!' And then, just to nail his sexist flag to the mast, the chief engineer complains about being disabled by their female host. 'If she ever does that to me again, I'm off women for life.'

At one point having gained control of the women, the pain collars no longer working on their burly captives, Kirk threatens Mea: 'I think our friend there would like to talk to you. Shall I have him take you out into the hall?' The implication here is that Kirk would throw Mea to the prisoner and be subjected to whatever revenge was on his mind. Kirk being complicit in female assault is distasteful in the extreme. And then there's the casual sexism of 'It made a surgeon out of her... and without this helmet I've got a hunch she wouldn't know enough to come in out of the rain.' This putdown is not justified, because at this stage the women are simply portrayed as naïve.

Kirk makes another sexist contribution to the resolution of the planet's sexes reacquainting themselves. 'Women have been civilising men for millions of years, all over the galaxy. It goes with the sex.' While this could be taken as a compliment, there's an undercurrent that suggests that this has been achieved through sexual manipulation.

It's disappointing that the 'pretty cool young woman' Lieutenant McAdams never made it to the final cut, as she would at least offer us a strong, compassionate, female character who could help Mea and her kind. Saying that, in the episode's coda it's joked that McAdams 'has provided the ladies with a tool for procuring furs and fuel from the men.' Perfume. And to further compound his simplistic resolution to a problem that the *Enterprise* crew have created with their interference, the captain suggests that 'I am not given to predictions, but I venture one now. That conflict on the surface will be a very short one.' Based on the fact that cuddling is warmer than sitting in front of a fire.

Was the removal of Gilliam, McAdams, Alexandrovich and Gilliam a tactic to cut costs, by reducing the outlay for additional actors? Setting the abduction on the standing set of the Bridge would also avoid the cost of having to build an asteroid set.

As a final observation on Script Draft 1, on Page 1 of the document, next to the title *Spock's Brain*, Lee Cronin has added, in brackets, '(Strongly recommend new title)'. This suggests the writer was dissatisfied with the pulpy title, which may have been used as a placeholder until something better came along. Why it wasn't changed is unknown, possibly the lack of anything better being suggested, or a greater focus elsewhere on more pressing matters.

Final Revised Draft: July 1, 1968

While this is the final draft, it's not what was used to film the episode, additional page revisions being added by Producer Fred Freiberger on 3, 5, 11 and 16 July 1968[133].

Comparing this version with the first draft, the first obvious change is that there is only a single life-reading on the alien vessel instead of three, and the intruder, now called Kara instead of Mea, beams herself straight onto the Bridge rather than being beamed across to the Transporter Room by the *Enterprise* crew. For the first time, Kirk suggests that Spock is brought with them on their mission, and the ticking clock of how long the Vulcan can survive has dropped from the initial week, then three days, to just 24 hours. Kirk is now convinced that if someone has the skill to remove Spock's brain, they will also have the ability to successfully re-attach it.

The *Enterprise* pursues the thief's ship's ion trail, locating her on one of three Class-M planets in the Sigma Draconis system. Kirk, Chekov, Scott and two security guards beam down to the surface, and having captured a local caveman-like male who shares his fear of the Others, the away team discover the entrance to an underground city. Kirk asks McCoy and Spock to beam down – the Vulcan being led by McCoy's remote-control device – and they descend, leaving Chekov and the security guards to stand guard.

Down in the underground lair, Kirk stuns a 'quite pretty' girl when she attempts to activate a device similar to the one on the *Enterprise*.

---

[133] Cushman, *These are the Voyages: TOS Season Three*, p182.

The girl, Luma, states they are not Morg or Eymorg and that 'I know nothing about a brain.' McCoy's tricorder identifies that she has the mind of a child. Scott picks up Spock's voice on a communicator channel and the away team are then overcome by Kara and two burly guards, themselves being controlled by chest bands. Kirk and his team awake, now also wearing pain bands, and confront Kara, Luma and other females, who are stroking sleek, well-behaved men They are terrified by Kirk and his team and cower in the corner, Kara activating the pain bands to disable them.

While under house arrest, Kirks asks Spock's voice to work out how to disarm their pain bands – it's the red button on Kara's device – and having escaped from captivity, is able to disarm their restraints. Kara confirms that Spock's brain could power the complex for 10,000 years to come. Kirk forces Kara to connect herself to the network via a helmet called the Teacher. With her improved intellect, Kara turns a phaser on Kirk, but she is disarmed and McCoy offers to use the knowledge-giving device to learn how to operate on Spock. The central control room is transformed into an operating arena. McCoy successfully reattaches Spock's brain, guided by Spock, who has had his vocal cords reattached, and the Vulcan delivers a closing speech explaining what caused the split in the society.

This version of the story is more familiar, closely resembling the completed episode. It also reflects some significant dumbing down – of the science, the logic and the women. It's frustrating that matters which were directly addressed in previous drafts have been removed, leaving holes in the plot. Why are they no longer using the universal translator? The locals surely don't speak English. Why are they not wearing the cold weather jackets of the previous draft? It's a freezing planet. And why is Chekov heating up a rock to keep himself and the redshirts warm? Can't they just ask for someone to beam down the jackets they forgot to bring? It's not like the scene in *The Naked Now* where Sulu cannot make contact with the ship and uses a similar method of warming up. In the absence of Gilliam and Alexandrovich, Chekov picks up some of their lines and gets a piece of the action, even saving the presumably costly sequence of traipsing 'across gullies, ridges and rocks.' Now he just points to the entrance to the underground lair, which is conveniently within metres of their landing spot.

And having taken the most useful tech out of the story – the universal translator – Spock communicates via communicator, though implausibly sounds just like Nimoy. This was addressed in the previous script – translated voices don't sound like the originator, and communicator signals surely cannot add the voice patterns of a disembodied brain,

Mea has become Kara and the other girl gains a name – Luma – but the indigenous females suffer in this draft. It's shocking that instead of trying to strike up some opening gambit with the latter, the first thing that Kirk does is stun her. And then there's the bizarre direction: 'They excitedly bend down over the body of the girl'. Why excitedly? Or what about the damning by faint praise of 'She is quite pretty'. Scott again shares some sexist insight: 'Could anything be simpler. When any menial work is needed, the women press the men into service.' Or 'There's no sign of genius in those women.' But the biggest victim here is the women's intellect. Instead of hiding what they've done, or admitting to it, these ladies simply have no idea what's going on.

McCoy's says of Luma 'Her mind is functioning on a very simple level.

Mental faculties down here have been almost atrophied through non-use.' Speaking in short, simple sentences, she has no idea what a brain is, let alone who stole Spock's brain. We're told that the other women observe the crew 'with child-like interest rather than with the mature excitement of women confronted with strange men.' They're easily flattered by Kirk and McCoy's charm, but show the 'sudden fury of a child' when challenged, 'cowering and terrified noises and cries are coming from them.' They are not strong women, they are hysterical, irrational and duplicitous, and maintain control through pleasure and pain. We're not certainly not on Nefel anymore.

Televised Version: September 28, 1968

The final, televised version is not significantly different to the Final Draft script. Words are rearranged in sentences and whole lines are swapped within a delivery, possibly where the actors struggled to get their lines right. There's an ongoing confusion as to whether they visit Sigma Draconis VI or VII. Uhura says that VII has the high energy generation, and this is the planet name-checked by Kirk and Uhura in the ship's log voice-over, but it's actually VI that they beam down to, as established earlier, when checking the full star system. This presumably just got missed during the production. A neat technical addition is Kirk telling the landing party to set their 'suit temperatures to 72.' A clever way to address why they aren't wearing jackets for the extreme weather, though Chekov still feels the need to phaser a rock for heat. Why not turn up the suit thermostat? Scott reads that there are four large humanoids in the area, and then five appear, presumably this Neanderthal having his own personal cloaking device, and instead of stroking their pet men, the women in the compound are feeding them multi-coloured food cubes as previously seen on the *Enterprise*.

The pain device has changed again. Instead of being collars (too similar to the devices in *The Gamesters of Triskelion* earlier in the year?), headbands or around their chests, we now have clunky belts. Kira is played as even more screechy, whiny and petulant than the previous script directed. Thankfully, the entire final scene on the *Enterprise* has been dropped, so we're saved the references to perfume and cuddles, or Vulcans propagating by mail. This also means we get even less discussion of what happens next to Kara and company.

Who made the changes?

So why were the changes made, and whose idea were they? Television production is a collaborative process, with changes made at any point on the entire journey, so it can be difficult to identify who came up with the new ideas along the way. However, we're fortunate that some of the creatives have been forthcoming in claiming credit (and at times accepting the blame) for the revisions to the story.

Executive Producer Robert H Justman confirms that he suggested to Producer Fred Freiberger 'Would it be three times as exciting to see three practically naked women as it would be to see only one of them?'[134], Freiberger himself added that the women '...should come off **extraordinarily beautiful.**'[135].

Margaret Armen, writer of **TOS** episodes *The Gamesters of Triskelion*,

---

[134] Cushman, *These are the Voyages: TOS Season Three*, p186.
[135] Cushman, *These are the Voyages: TOS Season Three*, p185 (emphasis in original).

The Paradise Syndrome and *The Cloud Minders*, added further insight into the understanding of Season 3's new Producer, Freiberger. 'I was in the projection room seeing an early episode, I've forgotten the reason, and Fred came in... He watched the episode with me, smoked a big cigar and said, 'Oh, I get it. Tits in space.' That didn't sit well with me at all...'[136]

During the script stage, Arthur H Singer joined the show as story consultant and in his memo to Freiberger of 2 April 1968 he supported the idea of changing '...passive little women to statuesque beautiful women with a superiority complex' and that they consider themselves to be an 'elite group'.[137]

With these examples, the Producer and Executive Producer are injecting ideas, presumably to 'sex-up' the story, while at the same diminishing the role of the women as previously written. Freiberger is not apologetic of his work, instead placing the blame on the originators of the stories. He later told William Shatner of the already-approved Gene L Coon and John Meredyth Lucas storylines that he was presented with when joining the show, including *Spock's Brain*:

> 'These were Roddenberry-approved storylines, written by the writer/producers of the first two seasons. I felt that surely this group knew the show and characters better than I did.'[138]

Freiberger was merely picking up material commissioned before his involvement and then running with it.

---

[136] Gross, Edward, 'Treks into Paradise', *Starlog #125*, December 1987.
[137] Cushman, *These are the Voyages: TOS Season Three*, p185.
[138] Shatner, *Star Trek Memories*, p265.

Spock's Brain was director Marc Daniels' only work on Season 3, the last of his 14 episodes for **TOS**. He recalled 'Fred Freiberger, the new producer, and I didn't agree on what the director's role was... They just want you to do the work, get the shots and forget the rest of it. I didn't particularly care for that kind of thinking.'[139]

This all contributes to the wider picture of a show being steered by a new captain with a different way of thinking to what had been previously established. And because of the reduced budget, directors also had less opportunity to go into paid overtime, thus having fewer hours to shoot the material. This ultimately results in less coverage and fewer takes from which to choose the best content at the editing stage.

It was during the filming of this episode that Roddenberry famously requested the addition of a new ending, set in the transporter room, where Uhura presents Spock with a Vulcan IDIC (Infinite Diversity in Infinite Combinations) medallion – essentially promoting a new piece of merchandise to be sold by his mail order Lincoln Enterprises venture. Freiberger vetoed the suggestion, but just imagine how even more unpopular this episode would have been if that scene had been shoehorned in here, rather than in the later *Is There in Truth No Beauty?* (1968)[140].

Meant to be funny?

It has been suggested that Coon was actually in agreement with the changes which were made to his script. He no longer had the influence to challenge them as he would have as a producer, so he

---

[139] Gross, Edward, 'Assignment: 'Trek'', *Starlog #114*, January 1987.
[140] Cushman, *These are the Voyages: TOS Season Three*, p194.

may have pragmatically let the current producers get on with it. Or maybe his script was a Trojan horse, designed to embarrass his former employers. William Shatner suggested this.

> 'Now rumour has it that Coon, who was constantly at odds with Roddenberry over the show's content, wrote this script as a practical joke, ribbing **Star Trek** for taking itself way too seriously. It just goes to show that practical jokes sometimes backfire.'[141]

But why would a writer do that? Coon would be burning his bridges for possible future work with the show's creatives.

David Gerrold doesn't think that Coon dropped the ball with the script.

> 'I don't think he deliberately set out to write that show seriously. I don't think there's any way you can take that episode seriously. You've got to take it as an in-joke. What's the stupidest science-fiction idea to do? What if somebody stole Spock's brain? Gene L Coon had that kind of sense of humour to do that kind of impish stuff. He had an irreverent sense of humour, and I think he wanted to poke **Star Trek** because someone was taking it too seriously.'[142]

This was seconded by D C Fontana: '[Coon] wrote *Spock's Brain*... which is usually reviled, but it was one of those episodes where he was actually having fun. He was jerking everybody's chain, and

---

[141] 'Star Trek Insight: *Spock's Brain*'.
[142] Gross, Edward and Mark A. Altman, *The Fifty-Year Mission: The First 25 Years*, pp205-6.

people took it seriously.'[143]

William Shatner added that '...Coon's most important contributions to **Star Trek** can be found in the humour that he infused into every script. Coon's comic interludes were met with immediate viewer enthusiasm and very quickly became an important element of the series.'[144]

This is first-hand testimony from people who worked with Coon, so maybe critics are just missing the joke.

'**Star Trek** had its share of bad episodes. In almost every case the fault can be traced to the scripts,' suggested Gerrold, citing *Spock's Brain* as one of four examples[145]. But the buck doesn't stop with the writer. 'If even the two top producers of the show could be responsible for weak scripts, the cause of **Star Trek**'s occasional (and in the third year, frequent) failures must be something other than just an occasional poor writer.'[146]

---

[143] Nazarro, Joe, 'The Other Gene' *Star Trek: Epic Episodes*, p58.
[144] Shatner, *Star Trek Memories*, p157.
[145] The other three were *The Alternative Factor* (1967), *The Omega Glory* (1968), and *Spectre of the Gun* (1968).
[146] Gerrold, *The World of Star Trek*, pp208-209.

CHAPTER 6: 'IF ONLY'
The Roddenberry Gene

The final line of dialogue of **TOS** is delivered by Kirk in *Turnabout Intruder*, lamenting that things could have been so much better for his old flame, Dr. Janice Turner. 'Her life could have been as rich as any woman's, if only. If only.'

Written by Gene Roddenberry, his sole teleplay for Season 3, this series swansong begs a line of thought. If only NBC had delivered on their promise of a 7:30pm slot on Mondays instead of changing it to 10pm on a Friday then, according to Roddenberry, he would have remained with the show. And if only Roddenberry had been showrunner, the quality of Season 3 might have been raised. And if only Roddenberry had been at the table, we might not have had such a sexist episode as *Spock's Brain*.

But are we really suggesting that if Roddenberry had been in charge, this would have prevented episodes like *Spock's Brain* from being made in the way that they were? This takes us from the territory of 'If only...' to 'What if...' and the answer is, of course, that this will never be known. But Roddenberry continued writing and producing content up until his death in 1991, so we have the opportunity to judge how his Season 3 might have looked through the lens of his post-**TOS** work. Would he have solved the problems or actually caused more?

Pretty Maids All in a Row (1971)

Written and produced by Roddenberry, and his sole theatrical movie credit, his first post-**TOS** film project was a campus-set comedy thriller starring Rock Hudson, Telly Savalas and Angie Dickinson, directed by *Barbarella*'s Roger Vadim. Hudson is counsellor 'Tiger' McDrew, who sleeps with his students, killing them when they outlive their usefulness or fall in love with him, while Savalas is the detective investigating the increasing body count. The opening scene follows student Ponce and his fetishised male gaze as he fixates on the bodies of his classmates, looking up their skirts and fixating on their chests. Simultaneously, counsellor Tiger is having sex with very young students, who are beguiled by his charm. We soon discover that he's the murderer, leaving one victim in the toilets with the sign 'So long, honey!' pinned to her chest. Consider the manner in which the predatory Tiger portrays one victim during police questioning by Captain Surcher.

TIGER

I think Jill fooled a lot of people. Not particularly intelligent. IQ of 103. She seemed more intelligent because she adapted so well to high school level activities.

SURCHER

Quite beautiful though.

TIGER

Yes, extraordinary figure. Excellent dancer, baton twirler.

SURCHER

What kind of men would a girl like this be attracted to, Tiger?

TIGER

Well, let me see. I'd say it's not impossible she had marriage in mind.

Two professionals, discussing a young girl who has been brutally murdered and yet their focus in on her beauty, her skills as a cheerleader, how adept she is at fooling people and whether her primary focus is on getting married. Other girls in the class – the 'Pretty Maids all in a row' – are depicted as sex-crazed, even flirting with the homicide detective. Angie Dickinson as the female lead, teacher Miss Smith, seduces young Ponce by luring him back to her apartment and bathing him. In this distasteful male fantasy, women are either sexualised teenage students or sexual predators. Director Vadim did not disguise his objectification of his topless 'Pretty Maids': 'Gretchen Burrell has the best figure in the cast; her breasts are just right, like a compromise between Jane Russell and Twiggy,' while 'a nude, Slavic woman weeping, to me, is irresistibly sexy.'[147]

Genesis II (1973)

Written and produced by Roddenberry, this was the pilot to a planned series featuring character Dylan Hunt[148], a 1970s scientist who awakens from suspended animation in 2133 to find that the world has regressed to a primitive civilisation following the Great Conflict. A strange concept is introduced where the method of reviving dormant subjects relies on the same chemicals that power a person's sex drive – the need to reproduce. We're never sure if the half-mutant Tyranian, Lyra-a played by Mariette Hartley (Zarabeth in **TOS'** *All our Yesterdays*) employs this manual stimulation to kick-start Dylan Hunt, but she's quick to strip down to her William Theiss-

---

[147] Vadim, Roger, 'Vadim's 'Pretty Maids' – pictorial essay', *Playboy*, Vol. 18, No. 4, April 1971.
[148] A name reused for **Gene Roddenberry's Andromeda**, a series made posthumously.

designed bikini to reveal a double navel, and 'tucks him in' at night.

We discover that 'animal lust destroyed this world and caused civilisation to fall...' leading to 'the battle between the sexes, aggression between male and female.' We're told that there are some communities in the women's country where men are tolerated only as pets, and there's a subservient slave class controlled by Stim Sticks that dispense pleasure and pain, in similar manner to *Spock's Brain*'s Eymorgs. Lyra-a is revealed to be the villain, trying to lure Hunt away from the pacifist PAX, the other female of note in the movie being Harper-Smythe, a rather vanilla potential love interest for Hunt. In Lyra-a, Roddenberry gives us another duplicitous woman who cannot love, and controls men through her sexuality and duplicity, with Harper-Smythe an androgynous, sexless, passive observer, her role in the story to be a foil to Hunt's sexual advances. In the final scene, when Harper-Smythe denies that she has made a pass at him, Hunt replies: 'Pity, I bet you've got a great pancreas.'

The Questor Tapes (1974)

Based on a story credited to Roddenberry, he would share the teleplay credit for this TV series pilot with *Spock's Brain* writer Gene L Coon, though it would be screened after Coon's death. It features Robert Foxworth as android Questor, who together with scientist Jerry Robinson is searching for his creator, evil genius Dr Vaslovik. The story strays into sexist territory when the couple travel to England and meet socialite Lady Helena Trimble (surely a name-check to **Star Trek** super-fan Bjo Trimble?) and Questor suggests that Robinson seduces their host to gain intelligence. After Robinson refuses this suggestion, Questor offers to do this himself, revealing that he is 'fully functional', a moment that would be echoed in **TNG**'s *The*

Naked Now (1987) as Data (who shares many character traits with Questor) is seduced by Tasha Yar.

We cut to the next day, wondering if Questor performed his duties, and discover that he didn't, because Lady Trimble is actually a superspy with a high-tech control room. What's insulting to the character is that she's assumed to be a courtesan, Questor quoting the works of French author Guy de Maupassant: 'the human female can be persuaded in ways much more powerful than the simple exchange of specie.'[149] While we might forgive the new-born Questor for applying 19th century sexism, Robinson, who should really know better, concurs: 'I suppose given the right relationship, any woman could be convinced that there's more to life than money.'

Planet Earth (1974)

As with **TOS**, Roddenberry was offered a second pilot for the same series, with this return to the world of **Genesis II**, while recasting Hunt and Harper-Smythe. Roddenberry is creator, story writer and co-screenplay writer with Juanita Bartlett, focusing on the woman's country referenced in the first movie. Hunt and Harper-Smythe embark on a rescue mission to the Confederacy of Ruth, a post-apocalyptic matriarchy where one of their scientists is being held with other drugged men who are being coerced into serving their mistresses. The sisterhood is led by **TNG**'s Diana Muldaur as Marg, wearing a William Theiss halterneck in a plot that bears strong similarities to a story idea from Roddenberry's original **TOS** proposal of 11 March 1964: 'The Pet Shop – Exactly duplicating St Louis, 1910, a city where women are so completely the masters that men have the status of pets.' This synopsis is also mirrored in the way the

---

[149] 'Specie' here is referring to a form of currency.

Eymorgs treat their Morg male slaves in *Spock's Brain*.

Hunt serves as our male everyman, questioning whether the society is an example of 'Women's lib or women's lib gone mad?' As an undercover prisoner, he gets the opportunity to seduce Marg through drink. She argues that 'In nature, the female is always dominant. When that natural order is reversed, men become the same vain quarrelsome little seed carriers who lied and postured and drove the whole world into destruction.' Dylan is pragmatic, countering that 'females in charge is no more upside down than our system was. Women's lib, men's lib. What do you say we dump 'em both, Marg? Are you for people's lib?'

By drugging their men, the 'breeders' are becoming infertile, thus placing the future of this society in doubt. When the war-like Kreegs invade, the men have no alternative but to rise up, to break their chains and protect the women. After the men have saved the day, they broker a bizarre understanding with their mistresses to remain as their servants, but voluntarily. Of ABC's reaction to the movie, Roddenberry said 'I think what they had in mind... would be "science fiction women" with long legs, silver costumes, and well-endowed. And after we shot it, they came in very upset and disappointed. They didn't realize that's not my kind of science fiction and I was surprised they thought I might do that kind.'[150]

Is this movie a warning of what happens when Women's Lib goes too far? Or is it a male sex fantasy where the viewer scoffs at the fragile leadership that relies on drugs to maintain order? It also plays to the

---

[150] Zsalay, Jeff, 'Gene Roddenberry: The Years Between, The Years Ahead'. *Starlog* #51, October 1981.

offensive suggestion that women just need a good man to sort them out, with Meg even saying at one point 'I'd like to see the male who could dominate me,' and possibly meaning it. Contrary to what Roddenberry states, the 'science fiction women' theme is very familiar in his work – domineering females ruling over their men through artificial control.

Spectre (1977)

This horror thriller was a TV pilot produced by Roddenberry, based on his own story, the screenplay shared with Samuel A Peeples (**TAS**, *Beyond the Farthest star* (1973)). Starring Robert Culp as former criminologist William Sebastian and Gig Young as disgraced Doctor Hamilton, they're invited to England to investigate whether or not supernatural events are happening at the Cyon estate. We meet master of the house, Sir Geoffrey, who admits to 'living openly what most men do in secret,' his maids being dressed in plunging negligees. When Ham wakes up in his guest room bed, he's joined by a maid, and then a leather-clad dominatrix (complete with riding crop) and a school girl who calls him 'daddy'. These kinky comedy moments feel forced, highlighting that the women in this film fall essentially into the polar opposites of the Madonna (plain 'old maid' Anitra, whose 'puritanical sensibilities' are offended by her brother's lifestyle) or the Whore (the fantasy seductress as maid, chauffer, housekeeper, topless participant in a black magic ritual or sexualised succubus). One peripheral character is white witch Lilith, Sebastian's house keeper, played by Majel Barrett. It's a shame she's only in the opening and closing scenes, as she's the only woman in the picture who isn't a stereotype.

Star Trek: The Motion Picture (1979)

The first **Star Trek** movie has its screenplay credited to Harold Livingston, based on Alan Dean Foster's **Star Trek: Phase II** story *In Thy Image*, so it would be outside of our remit to judge sexist elements in its writing if Roddenberry did not officially have direct input. However, there are still questions about his contributions to the script, which was subject to multiple redrafts by Livingston and Roddenberry. At various stages, Roddenberry pushed for shared screenplay credit. Harlan Ellison stated in his review of the movie: 'I know that Gene's name was removed from the screen credit five times, and finally he was taken to Writers Guild arbitration by Harold Livingston, who wound up with the credit.'[151] Regardless of how much dialogue he wrote, Roddenberry was still Producer and had a say in the creative decisions that were made. In fairness, most of its elements do not raise concerns about sexism or misogyny: Uhura, Rand and Chapel all have senior roles, and Bob Fletcher's Starfleet uniforms are unisex and not sexualised. The problems exist with Ilia, the new Deltan navigator played by Persis Khambatta. The actor, who was a former Miss India, features prominently in the movie's marketing material in a white mini-robe, adding some glamour to photos featuring her middle-aged co-stars. It's how she gets the robe, and why she remains in it for the rest of the movie, that raises the issues.

When she first boards the *Enterprise*, Ilia is in regular Starfleet uniform, but then she's abducted by an alien probe and returns later, naked, in a sonic shower cubicle. When Kirk, Spock and a security guard go to Ilia's quarters to meet her, we see little more than her

---

[151] Ellison, Harlan, 'Ellison Reviews TREK', *Starlog #33*, January 1980.

outline behind the shower screen, and then Kirk does a curious thing. He punches some buttons on a console and a short bathrobe and high-heeled shoes materialise around the naked body. Being generous to Kirk here, maybe this technology only dispenses bathrobes and heels, yet at no point afterwards is it suggested that she changes into something more appropriate or practical. The worst reading of this situation is that Kirk decided he'd rather see Ilia in something more provocative than a Starfleet uniform, and chose an outfit that would accentuate her body. The real-world reason for this clunky costume change was no doubt to get Khambatta in a sensual outfit to capitalise on her figure, but on the face of it, as a story point it just doesn't compute.

Roddenberry's take on this is included in the movie's 'making of' book: 'Throwaway clothes, Gene Roddenberry believes, is the future of the clothing industry... When the Ilia-probe materializes au naturel... If "Ilia" had wished to change clothing, her old costume would dissolve away, to be reprogrammed into a new costume, very similar to the way a person's molecules are broken down and reassembled in the transporter.'[152] This still doesn't explain why Kirk's default was a short robe.

In Roddenberry's early re-draft of *In Thy Image* dated 7 November 1977, Kirk says to Ilia 'I know that Deltan females are not wanton, hairless whores.' She laughs at this, and Kirk follows-up by asking 'Have you ever sexed with a human?'[153] These inappropriate, misogynistic comments would be lost in future drafts, but highlight Roddenberry's obsession with Ilia's sexuality and looks. His

---

[152] Sackett and Roddenberry, *The Making of Star Trek: The Motion Picture*, p122.
[153] Gross and Altman, *The Fifty-Year Mission: The First 25 Years*, p325.

excitement regarding the character is even more explicit in his novelisation of the movie, his only published book. He shares Kirk's male gaze when seeing Ilia in the shower. 'It was Ilia! Lovely, almost unbearably lovely in her nudity!' Whereas he presumably should be more concerned about a potentially lethal lifeform on his ship, he's distracted by a naked woman. 'Kirk found his eyes shifting from the tiny light glow to what seemed impossibly lovely, hard-tipped breasts, which were at this moment swinging around to point directly at him.'[154] Perhaps this euphoria should only be expected, considering Deltans' effect on humans: 'an unsuspecting human was likely to find himself in considerable sexual excitement without understanding why. It could be troublesome aboard a vessel, but it was usually worth it since Deltans were superb navigators.'[155]

At Khambatta's request, Roddenberry wrote a detailed back story for the character, again going into unnecessary and inappropriate sexual detail:

> 'On 114-Delta V, almost everything in life is sex-oriented –it is a part of every friendship, every social engagement, every profession. It is simply the normal way to relate with others there. Since constant sex is not the pattern of humans and others aboard this starship, Ilia has totally repressed this emotion drive.'[156]

---

[154] Roddenberry, Gene, *Star Trek: The Motion Picture – A Novel*, pp177-178.
[155] Sackett and Roddenberry, *Making of Star Trek: The Motion Picture*, p80.
[156] Sackett and Roddenberry, *Making of Star Trek: The Motion Picture*, p42.

The actor herself had issues with what was required of her.

> 'Persis's strict religious beliefs and conservative Indian upbringing were not in keeping with the script's call for her to be totally nude behind the shower door... She finally agreed to wear a thin skin-coloured body stocking, and the impression on film is virtually indistinguishable from the real thing.'[157]

But why would she need to be fully naked if she was behind a screen? This fascination with the male gaze of a fantasy woman is not balanced elsewhere with the descriptions or treatment of any of the males or 'non-lovely' women. She's the desirable woman that Kirk cannot have, an antiquated trope long past is sell-by date.

Star Trek: The Next Generation (1987-1994)

Roddenberry's final return to **Star Trek** was **The Next Generation**, a show that he created and for which he served as Producer during its first year. If any of his post-**TOS** work can give us an indication of how he might have approached the third season of **TOS**, this is most likely. Boasting a new crew and a new *Enterprise*, their ongoing mission was 'to boldly go where no **one** has gone before', a gender-neutral directive that on the face of it suggested a more contemporary approach[158].

---

[157] Sackett and Roddenberry, *Making of Star Trek: The Motion Picture*, p162.
[158] It has been speculated that a line in *Introduction to Outer Space President's Science Advisory Committee, March 26, 1958* is the inspiration for the phrase: 'Where no man has gone before.' It reads: '...the thrust of curiosity that leads men to try to go where no one has gone before.' Whether or not it really was the inspiration has

With three female main cast members, Roddenberry was also increasing feminine representation, although of the three actors in these roles, only Marina Sirtis, as Deanna Troi, would be returning for the second year, and she'd still be in non-regulation uniform.

The Writer/Director's Guide is a good source to judge the show's intentions, and whether Roddenberry was addressing sexual equality. In 'What has not changed' we're reassured of 'The same "Band of Brothers" feeling (And sisters too, of course!).' But concerns creep in with the biographies of the female characters. Troi's description begins with 'An attractive and very witty Starfleet professional', while Crusher is 'An extremely attractive woman...,' this before we're informed that: 'she's one of the most talented and insightful physicians in Starfleet,' and that she has a: '**very** female form.' At one stage, in the eight-page preliminary series bible dated 11 May 1986, Troi was a 'four-breasted, oversexed hermaphrodite,' who would 'engage in almost constant sexual activity.'[159] And of Crusher, the original casting call of 17 March 1987 revealed: 'If it were not for her intelligence, personality, beauty, and the fact that she has a natural walk of a striptease queen, Capt. Picard might not have agreed to her request that Wesley observe bridge activities.'[160] Little appears to have changed in the 20 years since the Captain's Yeoman was described in the **TOS** series proposal as having: 'a strip-queen figure that even a uniform cannot hide.'

Of Tasha Yar, the **TNG** Writer/Director's Guide tells us she has the 'quality of conditioned-body beauty that would have flabbergasted

---

never been confirmed.
[159] Engel, Joe, *Gene Roddenberry: The Myth and the Man Behind Star Trek*, p213.
[160] 'Original Casting Call'.

males of a few centuries earlier' and manages to 'bring just an exciting sensual and intellectual challenge to males who enjoy (win or lose) full equality between the genders.' And then we're informed that Riker 'is intellectually committed to sexual equality... but he hasn't lived long enough to understand how completely different the two sexes can be. He's not fully aware that human females have needs of their own.' While the issue of gender parity is being addressed, nowhere are the male characters described by their looks. It's within this environment that such a sexist season 1 episode as *Angel One* (1987) would be made.

In *Angel One*, the away team beams down to: 'a matriarchal society where the female is as aggressively dominant as the male gender was on Earth hundreds of years ago.' It has evolved 'into a constitutional oligarchy. It is governed by a parliamentary body consisting of six elected Mistresses.' On the planet, Riker is soon at loggerheads with leader Beata, finally seducing her, but not before he has changed into local costume, bearing his left breast. The politics are muddled, the women's motives are unclear, and it's sexist in the way that Riker and the men create a solution where one was not even asked for. 'For a man, you can be very clever, Commander Riker,' Beata purrs patronisingly to Riker at the end of the episode, gender reversing the sort of comment that all-too-many women had heard, and yet saying nothing new about it.

TOS Producer Herbert J Wright was co-producer on **TNG** Season 1 (and part of Season 5) and recalls a pre-production meeting about *Angel One*, wary that as a trope, the concept of a matriarchal society had been overdone.

'So one of the major issues that we didn't want to do was an

Amazon Women kind of thing where the women are six feet tall with steel D cups... [but] everything that Gene got involved with had to have sex in it. It's so perverse that it's hard to believe. The places it was dragged into is absurd. We were talking about how women would react, and Gene was voicing all the right words again, saying, "Oh, yes, we've got to make sure that women are represented fairly, because, after all, women are probably the superior sex anyway, and it's real important we don't get letters from feminists, because we want to be fair and we don't want to infer that women have to rule by force if they do rule, because men don't have to rule by force." Very sensible stuff. All of a sudden something kicks in and he changes: "However, we also don't want to infer that it would be a better society if women ruled."'[161]

Denise Crosby described how she felt sexual equality manifested itself on the show:

> 'the intentions were good, but they should have taken it even further – that was my main frustration with the show. I hate to burst your bubble, but it was the writers, not Gene Roddenberry, who were fighting to make the female characters more dynamic. There was a real friction with putting the women in power.'

On why she asked to leave the show in mid-season, she confirmed that 'sexism was involved, and although I understand it is an inherent part of the world, it is something we must continue to fight. One day Gene Roddenberry told me, "This is the formula for *Star Trek* and it

---

[161] Gross and Altman, *The Fifty-Year Mission: The Next 25 Years*, p83.

works. It is not going to change.'"[162]

For all Roddenberry's alleged good intentions during this first year on the show, by the end of the season **TNG** had lost Denise Crosby, and Gates McFadden had been sacked, leaving only Marina Sirtis' Troi of the original trio, still in her revealing costume and in a traditional female 'caring' role. While McFadden would return in Season 3 and Troi would eventually gain a Starfleet uniform, the perceived equal treatment of women was not there yet. And as a parting thought, Wesley Crusher was initially to be a young girl, Leslie, but this was vetoed because Gene Roddenberry thought 'it might be a little bit of a stretch for today's audience to believe that a young female would have passionate feelings about matter and energy.'[163] As sexist suggestions go, that's a great insult to all female scientists, and endemic of the skewed equality in **TNG**.

Unproduced work

Of his unproduced work post-**TOS**, there are further examples of Roddenberry's ongoing fascination with sexualised fantasy females and gender politics. In her book about her relationship with Roddenberry, his former secretary Susan Sackett describes a moment from his partially-written novelisation of the script for the planned **Star Trek** movie *The God Thing*: '[T]here was a scene in which several female sirens tantalised Captain Kirk while they engaged in a weightless free-for-all, rolling in oil, their bodies glistening in what began as a sensual gymnastic event for Kirk...'[164]

---

[162] Stratford, Jennifer Juniper, 'Off Hollywood – Denise Crosby'.
[163] Sackett, Susan, *Inside Trek: My Secret Life with Star Trek Creator Gene Rodenberry*, location 2,471.
[164] Sackett, *Inside Trek,* location 1,292.

She also talks of the screenplay to *The Disappearance* that Roddenberry was working on with George Pal, about a world where 'women were helpless without men ... the men were lonely without women but got their sexual fixes from artificial companions.'[165]

We can also read about writer Morris Chapnick's experience when working with Roddenberry on a movie script based on Edgar Rice Burroughs' Tarzan:

> '[T]he natives sacrifice ten of the most beautiful women to a creature who came alive at that time. They had to be the most beautiful, the most exotic, the sexiest, and of course they had to wear very skimpy costumes. I'm sure this had to be Gene's thing - they all had to be in individual cages. Gene's fantasy, I guess.'[166]

He continues that 'a well-known writer was approached to "fix" the end of the script ... toning down both Tarzan's and Gene's hormones.'[167]

While, in the preceding examples, the focus has been on Roddenberry's writing, the themes he demonstrates on the page were also echoed in his public, personal attitudes. When talking about sexual equality on **TOS** in 1976 he told a live audience 'You cannot write in science fiction... without realising that sexual equality is as basic as any other kind of equality.' He paused for applause. 'This does not mean that in future pictures I will ever stop using women as sex objects, because I will not, but to be fair, we have always used

---

[165] Sackett, *Inside Trek,* location 1,567.
[166] Alexander, David, *Star Trek Creator: The Authorized Biography of Gene Roddenberry*, p359.
[167] Alexander, *Star Trek Creator*, p362.

and will be continuing to use males as sex objects too.' His logic seemed to be that provided men are treated as sex objects too, his sexualisation of women is an acceptable form of sex equality. He justified this further by saying that 'I've been used as a sex object myself. I think it's great fun,'[168] thus missing the point that using a female as sex object is a very different proposition to using a man, because the latter typically maintains their position of power and is doing something more than being vulnerable.

This version of Roddenberry is one perpetuated by those who worked with him, including Leonard Nimoy, though he suggested that he did change: 'His attitude toward women on **Trek** were miniskirted, big-boobed sex objects – toys for guys. He cleaned up the act gradually only because people pointed it out to him.'[169] In a series of interviews carried out shortly before the stroke that would lead to a significant deterioration in his health, Roddenberry was more reflective: 'I've learned to appreciate females very much... but I didn't start off appreciating them. I was a writer who believed that men were more logical than women. Now I don't think they're more logical... I do not consider males mentally superior to women. Physically, perhaps.'

He continued 'I am pleased with myself that I have evolved to appreciate women as much as men... Their femaleness is not a sign of weakness - we have very powerful women on **The Next Generation**.'[170] This softening was also reflected in Roddenberry's July 1983 letter to his cousin Julien: 'I now find myself feeling a bit

---

[168] *Inside Star Trek: The Enterprise Runs Aground.*
[169] Gross and Altman, *The Fifty-Year Mission: The First 25 Years*, p37.
[170] Fern, Yvonne, *Gene Roddenberry, The Last Conversation (Portraits of American Genius)*, p202.

ashamed of some of my past attitudes and action on the subject – perhaps much as others have been ashamed of their past attitudes about the blacks.'[171]

On the basis of the themes and examples identified in his post-**TOS** work, it seems unlikely that if Roddenberry had remained with the show on Season 3, episodes like *Spock's Brain* would have been any less sexist or misogynistic. If anything, and contrary to what he personally protested, the controlling, manipulative and mentally inferior women of *Spock's Brain* would likely be present in the way that these themes would be echoed in his own subsequent work. **TNG** was an example of what **Star Trek** would look like with Roddenberry at the helm, and as its first season demonstrated, its sexual politics were no less problematic than those of its 60s forebear.

---

[171] Alexander, *Star Trek Creator*, p474.

CHAPTER 7: FUTURE IMPERFECT
A Different Look at the 2250s and 2260s

Hundreds of hours of new **Star Trek** content have been produced for TV and cinema since *Spock's Brain*, giving us ample opportunity to see whether the problems of sexism and objectification apparent in *Spock's Brain* have since been addressed, and hopefully consigned to history. It's beyond the scope of this study to look at all post-*Spock's Brain* content through this lens, and instead the focus must be on **Star Trek** set in the 2250s and the 2260s, aboard the *Enterprise*. As this is the timeframe of **TOS**, we can compare the treatment of 1960s female characters with those in the show's later iterations. Did **The Animated Series** take the opportunity to dispense with matriarchal societies, did J J Abrams' *Star Trek* movies stop the objectification of women, and how does the new Number One fare in **Discovery**? As we'll see, it's a mixed bag of successes and failures.

The Animated Series (1973-1974)

Kirk's opening voiceover of Filmation's animated spinoff of **TOS** informs us that we're still on the 'five-year mission', which means we can feel safe placing it in the 2260s. The main crew are mostly the same as before, though with the addition of Edosian Lieutenant Arex (voiced by James Doohan) and female Caitian comms officer M'Ress (Nichelle Nichols) – budget constraints would require this doubling up, and also mean that Walter Koenig's Chekov was no longer on the bridge. Although she typically served as relief for Uhura and Spock when they were incapacitated or on away missions, M'Ress was a welcome additional female character, joining Uhura and Chapel as series regulars.

Produced for transmission during the children's Saturday morning TV slot, the half-hour shows would have less time than **TOS** to tell a story, but still tackled a number of interesting sci-fi themes, attracting writers of the calibre of Larry Niven and returning **TOS** scriptwriters Samuel L Peeples, D C Fontana, David Gerrold and Stephen Kandel. Another returning writer was Margaret Armen, her sole script for **TAS** being *The Lorelei Signal*, which signifies the best and worst examples of how sexism was prevalent in this updated incarnation of the show.

The crew of the *Enterprise* discover another matriarchal society, who this time lure men to their planet in the Taurean system every 27.346 star years to replenish themselves. Instead of an obedience collar or *Spock's Brain*-style pain belt, the men are controlled by conductor headbands that drain their life force. Immediately, McCoy suggests (presumably non-scientifically) that these are 'the most beautiful women in the galaxy.' As with *Spock's Brain*, a schism has separated the men from their women but, on this planet, the women have adapted by draining the life out of their men and now fuel themselves through the men who respond to their siren song. The all-male away team, wearing life-draining headbands, are aging at the rate of 10 years a day, and it's up to a female-led team commanded by Uhura to rescue them. The aging process is reversed and plans are made to take the women to a new planet.

In this animated story the women again control by force rather than persuasion. They are seductively dressed (as much as a children's show will allow), manipulative and they hope for 'New learning. Perhaps love. Oh, it is a much better future than immortality.' These are female killers who initially drained their own males of their life (the sexist implications are barely hidden). Their leader, Theela, explains that: 'the women's bodies developed a glandular secretion, enabling them to survive and to manipulate certain areas of the males' brains.' And they lament that: 'We are unable even to bear children.' While a fair point, it plays into the whole 'women just need love and to build a family' stereotype.

The one positive in this episode is Uhura's opportunity to shine. She takes control of the *Enterprise*, leads the landing party, stuns Theela and her accomplices and finds the dying crew members. Uhura has never had such agency before. Lou Scheimer, producer of **TAS**, recalled Nichelle's Nichol's reaction. 'During the table read of the script... where Uhura got to take command of the *Enterprise*, Nichelle yelled happily, "What? You're kidding! I actually get to run the *Enterprise*?"'[172]

However, this promotion of Uhura's role is tempered – most of her actions are led by Spock. He comes up with the solutions, from beaming down an all-female party, to summoning (who is still mooning after the Vulcan like a love-struck teenager) to him telepathically, to instructing the use of electromagnetic deflectors to block the signal from the planet, to reprogramming the transporter to reverse the accelerated ageing. It's Uhura's moment, yet she's just following orders from a male. And just to show that normal service has been resumed by the end, Uhura plays to the vanity of the once-again youthful Kirk by reassuring him, unprompted, that: 'You're more handsome than ever.'

The story bears many similarities to the story synopsis of *The Venus Planet,* included in a list of possible story ideas by Roddenberry in his

---

[172] Scheimer, Lou with Andy Mangels, *Lou Scheimer: Creating the Filmation Generation*, p99.

'Star Trek is...' **TOS** pitch of 11 March 1964:

> '...the very human male members of our crew find what seems the ultimate in amorous wish-fulfilment in the perfectly developed arts of this place of incredibly beautiful women. Until they begin to wonder what happened to all of the men there.'

This may be why the story feels so outdated, possibly being based on a 10-year-old pitch that was already an established sci-fi trope. And just to add a further *Spock's Brain*-related credential to the episode, the authors of *Star Trek 101* bestowed their Spock's Brain Award to this instalment for being the worst episode of the series.[173] As a whole, **TAS** was a positive extension of **TOS**, but it was not immune to the sexism previously exhibited in its forebear.

Deep Space Nine: Trials and Tribble-ations (1996)

A more positive light on sexism on the *Enterprise* in the 2250s and 2260s, post-**TOS** is shone by DS9's *Trial and Tribble-ations*, which takes some of the station's crew in the *Defiant* back in time to participate in the events of **TOS** episode *The Trouble with Tribbles* (1967). The original episode offers nothing troubling from a sexism perspective, actually providing Uhura with some off-duty scenes that show her playful side. This episode marked the 30th anniversary of **TOS**, and the integration of the current cast into footage of the original is designed to evoke nostalgia linked to this celebration.

Commander Sisko steps out in a bronze command top: 'In the old days, operations officers wore red, command officers wore gold,' he

---

[173] Erdmann, and Block, *Star Trek 101*, p48.

explains. And then Dax steps out in her red minidress and performs a pirouette: 'And women wore less.' Bashir and O'Brien are awestruck by their colleague's apparel, Julian throwing in the line: 'I think I'm going to like history!' Starfleet uniforms of this era can't really be that much of a surprise to Bashir – the assumption is that he's just stunned by this new look for Dax. It's sexist, it's inappropriate, and yet it feels wholly appropriate in this context. This is a knowing pastiche that's deliberately exaggerating the characters' behaviour.

While sharing a lift with the attractive Lieutenant Watley, O'Brien and Bashir are told that she is 'coming into Sickbay tomorrow for [her] physical. Fifteen hundred.' She leaves the men with their mouths open. 'You realise, of course, she's just using you to get to me,' suggests O'Brien, though at this stage Julian is more worried that he's lusting after his own great grandmother and in danger of creating a predestination paradox. It's fun, it's awkward, it's deliberately throwing a light on what would have passed as acceptable in the 1960s, while also telling us that we've come a long way since then. To complete the Sixties feeling, there's also a waitress in a colourful Theiss-inspired outfit with a plunging neckline. One final moment of fun is Dax's moment of hero worship.

> DAX
>
> He's so much more handsome in person. And those eyes.
>
> SISKO
>
> Kirk had quite the reputation as a ladies' man.
>
> DAX
>
> Not him. Spock.

Star Trek (2009)

Warping past *The Motion Picture*, which has already been covered in chapter 6, the next available evidence is provided by JJ Abrams' 21st century big screen relaunch of **Star Trek**, mainly set nearly a decade before **TOS** in 2258. The main bridge crew of **TOS** return, though the opportunity to include Rand is not taken and Chapel only exists as an off-screen voice. This means that the sole female member of the main cast is Uhura, played by Zoe Saldana, who we first meet in a bar with a drunk Kirk hitting on her. From the outset we're assured of her intelligence – she's studying xenolinguistics – and her confidence in the way she handles Kirk. Throughout the movie she's doing more than just opening hailing frequencies; she's intercepting and translating key messages, though she's not involved in any action sequences. There's a running gag about her not revealing her first name to Kirk[174] – she stubbornly refuses to tell it to him directly – and the addition of a romance between her and Spock.[175]

Other female characters are treated well, from Spock's mother Amanda, to members of the bridge crew and an alien doctor. Less savoury is a scene in a dorm room where a topless Kirk and green-skinned Orion student Gaila in her underwear are in bed, and Kirk suddenly hides when her roommate Uhura enters. We then have an awkward moment where Kirk is the unexpected voyeur to Uhura

---

[174] This is presumably poking fun at **TOS** or the **Star Trek** movies, where she is never addressed by a first name.
[175] In **TOS**, there is no romantic relationship between Uhura and Spock. She sings about him as accompaniment to his Vulcan lute-playing in *Charlie X* (1996), and asks of him in *The Man Trap* (1966): 'Why don't you tell me I'm an attractive young lady, or ask me if I've ever been in love?'

stripping down to her underwear. Presumably a call-back to the Kirk trope of 'a girl on every planet', the moments with Gaila show a consenting relationship where the Orion is clearly in charge, a more positive reading of the females of this race who are often portrayed as slaves. More troubling is Kirk's male gaze as he spies on Uhura, in a moment that feels like it's been added as frat humour.

Female Starfleet crew in the movie predominantly wear minidresses, a redesign of the Theiss original by Michael Kaplan. As noted in chapter 2, Saldana approved of the iconic dress as it helped quickly familiarise her with the character. A positive element of the movie is the use of Uhura on its main poster alongside Kirk and Spock. While this was designed to capitalise on Zoe Saldana's rising stardom (she would appear as female lead Neytiri later that year in James Cameron's *Avatar* (2009)), Uhura was also sharing a poster with her two male leads, a positive step towards equality.

Star Trek Into Darkness (2013)

Even before the movie had been released, *Into Darkness*' director, JJ Abrams, warned that '**Star Trek** has to be sexy. That's in keeping with the original spirit of the series... Hey, it wouldn't be **Star Trek** if there weren't some hot young actors, women and men, in various moments of either undress or flirtation.' He continued 'We have Alice Eve joining us; she's an incredibly wonderful, versatile actress and definitely in the sexy category. She's a great complement to Uhura.' Abrams concluded, 'it's always fun playing the womanising card with Kirk and seeing him in bed with girls who might not be completely human...'[176]

---

[176] Hochman, David, 'Playboy Interview: J J Abrams', Playboy Vol. 60,

The sequel to *Star Trek (2009)* would generate considerable online debate for many reasons, one of which is significant to our study. While some factions of fandom were concerned about the re-use of **TOS** villain Khan, others were disappointed by the twisted revision of *The Wrath of Khan'* (1982) that this time saw Kirk sacrificing himself rather than Spock. However, much of the ire was aimed at a scene involving Alice Eve's Carol Marcus and the subsequent response to the criticism from the film-makers.

The positives first: Uhura continues to play an important role, being in the heart of the action on the away team as the movie opens. She has problems with her relationship with Spock, leads discussions with some Klingons on their home world of Qo'noS (before stabbing one) and beams down to help Spock during the movie's climax on Earth. The addition of a secondary female character, Carol Marcus, is also (on the face of it) a positive move to increase the number of female characters in the movie. This legacy character from *The Wrath of Khan* is presented as a strong, educated character with a specialism in advanced weaponry. She even patronises Kirk: 'You're much cleverer than your reputation suggests, Captain Kirk,' and is incredulous that he can't remember who Christine Chapel is.

But then there's the underwear scene. The warning was there in the international trailer[177] for the movie, which included a brief shot of Alice Eve in her underwear. With no context, it was part of the montage of clips to encourage potential viewers to watch the movie. In the final film, Kirk and Doctor Marcus are in a shuttlecraft on the *Enterprise*, discussing how best to disarm torpedoes. She tells Kirk to

---

No. 4.
[177] *'Star Trek Into Darkness* – International Trailer – United Kingdom'.

look away as she strips out of her Starfleet uniform to change into a flight suit. Kirk, being Kirk, sneaks a peek and sees Marcus in her bra and panties, and she asks him to turn away, this time with mock indignation. It's a brief moment and adds nothing to the movie beyond sharing Kirk's male gaze at an attractive young lady in her underwear. It's pure, gratuitous objectification – Marcus' credentials and value as a subject expert are at this point stripped away with her miniskirt. It feels like one of the excesses of **TOS** has been resurrected in the 21st Century, but not this time as an ironic throwback.

When asked about this scene by MTV reporter Josh Horowitz, co-writer Damon Lindelof replied:

> 'Why is Alice Eve in her underwear, gratuitously and unnecessarily, without any real effort made as to why in God's name she would undress in that circumstance? Well there's a very good answer for that. But I'm not telling you what it is. Because… uh… MYSTERY?'

He added that there was also a scene featuring Benedict Cumberbatch's Harrison/Khan in the shower, 'but I don't think it ever got shot[178]. You know why? Because getting actors to take their clothes off is DEMEANING AND HORRIBLE AND... Oh. Right. Sorry.'[179]

Lindelof's jokey and confusing reply understandably created further discussion on social media, leading to him posting a Tweet, which he later deleted:

> 'I copped to the fact that we should have done a better job of

---

[178] Despite Lindelof's claim, this scene **was** shot, because JJ Abrams shared footage of it.
[179] Josh Horowitz, Josh, '*Star Trek Into Darkness* Spoiler Special: Your Questions Answered'.

not being gratuitous in our representation of a barely clothed actress. We also had Kirk shirtless in underpants in both movies. Do not want to make light of something that some construe as mysogenistic [sic]. What I'm saying is I hear you, I take responsibility and will be more mindful in the future. Also, I need to learn how to spell "misogynistic."'[180]

His reply has echoes of Gene Roddenberry's earlier response to an accusation of women being used as sex objects: 'I've been used as a sex object myself. I think it's great fun.' Here we're being told that because Kirk takes his shirt off or Harrison is seen in the shower, it justifies semi-naked women. But can one be compared equally with the other?

When Abrams appeared on Conan O'Brien's late night chat show on 23 May 2013, he addressed the charges of sexism in the scene.

'The intent was, it's Kirk, who was always a womanizing character. So the idea was, have a beat like that amidst all this action and adventure. He looks and then looks away. I don't think I quite edited the scene in the right way ... Some people see it as exploiting her, and while she is lovely, I can also see their point of view.'

He then shared the clip of Harrison/Khan in the shower, to suggest that this was squaring things up.[181] The scene in the trailer with Eve in her underwear would be further exploited by having a hidden website link in it. Presumably it was anticipated that this particular

---

[180] Ben Child, *'Star Trek Into Darkness* Writer Apologises for Underwear Scene'.
[181] Unknown, 'EXCLUSIVE: J J Abrams Shows a Deleted *Star Trek Into Darkness* Scene'.

scene in the trailer would be paused, and whilst there, the viewer could unlock a previously-unseen poster.[182]

At the time of the movie's home entertainment release, another of its co-writers, Alex Kurtzman, weighed in on whether the scene with Marcus was justified:

> 'Ultimately, I think it's one of those things that you either accept is part of the scene dynamic – you know, she is bold, and certainly Carol Marcus as we knew her was bold from the first movie. And we figured, how do we harness the spirit of that in this scene, and that's ultimately where we came to it from. But certainly it's been criticized as egregious, and I guess everybody has their own point of view of that. All I can tell you is that it's not something we went into blindly, and certainly we all sat in a room going, okay, we're going to be criticized for this, but how do we justify this in a way that feels like it was thought about? And either you go for it or you don't.'[183]

The responses from Abrams, Lindelof and Kurtzman are disappointing, not just because they come across as insincere, but because they equate partial male nudity with partial female nudity. Kurtzman's response is more considered, but is still not apologetic. It's an interesting perspective, because Marcus' boldness does **not** come across in this scene as it is seen in the final movie. The intentions might have been there but the execution suggests

---

[182] Pascale, Anthony, 'Trailer Easter Eggs Lead To New *Star Trek Into Darkness* International Poster Artwork'.
[183] Gilchrist, Todd, 'Star Trek's Alex Kurtzman Talks Khan, Kirk's Journey and Carol Marcus' Underwear'.

something different, and it's the gratuitous shot of Eve in her underwear that the scene will ultimately be remembered for, not her boldness.

The movie's costume designer, Michael Kaplan, revealed much about his director's tastes and intentions. 'Zoe Saldana looked pretty stunning in her red wetsuit, JJ's favourite costume. It was a big success putting her in a red wetsuit... Last time, Zoe needed to wear underwear, and this time it was Alice Eve's turn. You know, it's a rather large male fanbase, and JJ wanted to appeal to that.'[184] Of the film's retro costumes, he explained: 'I wanted the film based in the 60s... Not literally the 60s, but I wanted my thinking to be grounded in the concept of the original **Star Trek**, almost like an homage.' And of Carol Marcus' underwear: 'After trying my hand at reinventing the bra, the results were so distracting that the intent of the scene would have been missed. I will say no more...'[185] It's not just the 60s look that had been revived, it's the objectification too.

A final (dis)honourable mention must go to McCoy in this movie, who is sexist in Carol's presence. He's with Marcus, preparing to disarm a torpedo. He whispers aloud aside to Kirk: 'You know when I dreamt about being stuck on a deserted planet with a beautiful woman? There was no torpedo.' Kirk reminds him that he's not there to flirt. Bones also calls Carol 'sweetheart' in the most patronising way. McCoy was not averse to this sort of occasional bad behaviour in the **TOS**, but mapping this trait onto the 21st century version is a jarring

---

[184] Godfrey, Alex, '*Star Trek Into Darkness*: How it was Made, By the People Who Made it'.
[185] Laverty, Lord Christopher, 'Costume Designer Michael Kaplan on *Star Trek Into Darkness*'.

choice.

Star Trek Beyond (2016)

The movie released in **Star Trek**'s 50th anniversary year featured a new director to the franchise in Justin Lin and new writers in Simon Pegg (who also plays Mr Scott) and Doug Jung. The sexism of *Into Darkness* has gone, and instead we have a movie with multiple strong female characters, led by Sofia Boutella's Jaylah. This is not a woman waiting to be rescued, instead she's the one rescuing stranded members of the *Enterprise* crew. A formidable engineer, she manages to get the abandoned USS *Franklin* up and running and has developed some ingenious image refractors to assist her in battle.

Initially she sits in the command chair on the *Franklin*'s bridge, much to Kirk's chagrin, and yet she is the one who's probably most deserving of the honour. Kirk tells her 'All I know is we stand a better chance with you,' and he's right. Her acceptance into Starfleet at the end of the movie is a worthy reward.

Ensign Syl is a female of an unspecific species with cranial appendages in which she can hide a vital component of the Abronath weapon. She's disintegrated when the movie's villain Krall demonstrates the power of the weapon. Kalara is a mutated human who poses as alien in distress to lure Kirk into exposing his location to Krall and there's a new female alien bridge crew member called Tyvanna.

Uhura has much to do in the movie, including dealing with the end of her relationship with Spock, and successfully completes the actions required to separate the saucer section of the *Enterprise*.

After she's captured by Krall, she attempts to send a distress call and aids Jaylah and Scotty in disrupting the alien Swarm's frequency while en route to attacking the Yorktown base. As with the other women in the movie, she's treated with respect, there's no objectification, and she's truly an equal among her peers. After *Into Darkness*, this is a palette cleanser, its treatment of women far more aligned with modern sensibilities than its 2013 predecessor. Dropping its use of outdated stereotypes and misjudged objectification, this presented a more desirable and credible future, rather than riffing on past glories.

Star Trek: Discovery (2017-) and Star Trek: Short Treks (2018-20)

Volumes could be written (and surely will be) on the positive depiction of women on **Discovery** – from Michael Burnham to Philippa Georgiou – and that's before we acknowledge the show's progressive use of transgender and non-binary characters, respectively with Gray and Adira. But for the purposes of this study, our focus is on the *Enterprise* and its adventures.

The *Enterprise* makes a surprise appearance in 2258 at the end of **Discovery**'s series 1 finale, *Will You Take My Hand?* (2018), though we don't meet Captain Pike until Season 2 opener *Brother* (2019), and it isn't until *Such Sweet Sorrow* (2019) that we board his vessel and get to meet the crew. Number One is at the helm, Lieutenant Amin is navigating. We see a crew of mixed sex and races in uniforms that are variants of those seen in *The Cage* and *Where No Man Has Gone Before*, females wearing either trousers or skirts with knee-high boots.

We discover in *Such Sweet Sorrow, Part 2* (2019) that Pike's executive officer (or XO), Number One, has been given a name in this series – Una[186]. As well as being a play on the word used for the number one in some languages (un, uno) it helps humanise the character, distancing her from the 'glacierlike' Number One of *The Cage*. In *An Obol for Charon*, Pike describes her to Burnham: 'Number One is very resourceful. People have a tendency to end up owing her favours.' We meet her in this episode when she catches up with Pike on the *Discovery*, smiling when she reveals that she second-guessed what he was going to say. This suggests a woman with a good sense of humour and a familiarity with her captain. She tells him what she has discovered about Spock, not disclosing the unsanctioned channels she used, thus protecting Pike and showing that she is willing to bend the rules when required. As they part, Pike tells her 'As usual, we agree,' and in her farewell she wishes him to keep safe. In this short sequence we're already getting a strong sense of Una's character, her loyalty and her abilities.'

The most time spent with Una is in **Short Trek**'s *Q&A* (2019) which follows Spock's first day on the *Enterprise*, where he first meets Number One. She encourages him to ask questions, which continue while they're stuck in a turbolift, waiting to be rescued. She recommends to Spock, on seeing him smiling: '...if you want to command, you're gonna have to learn to keep your freaky to yourself. Even if that's painful.' Una then reveals her own 'freaky' by performing *I Am the Very Model of a Modern Major-General* from

---

[186] Number One was first referred to as Una in the 2016 *Star Trek: Legacies* novel trilogy series, its authors Greg Cox, David Mack, Dayton Ward and Kevin Dilmore acknowledging that this is in honour of **Star Trek** (and **Black Archives**) author Una Cormack. https://twitter.com/DavidAlanMack/status/1119428330674114561.

Gilbert and Sullivan's **The Pirates of Penzance**. As they are rescued from the turbolift, she makes Spock promise to never reveal this secret.

We now have a clearer understanding of this character – her technical knowledge, her wish to share advice, her professionalism and her vulnerabilities... and that dry wit again. We even know a little more about Lieutenant Amin who rappels down the turbolift to rescue them: 'She's a champion climber and she's ready to go.'

Pike, Spock and Number One will return as the leads of **Star Trek: Strange New Worlds**, scheduled to launch in 2022. Very little is known about the show at this time beyond that it will be set in the years before Captain Kirk boarded the *Enterprise*, and follow its crew as they explore new worlds around the galaxy. During a panel for **Strange New Worlds** on **Star Trek** Day (8 September 2021) to commemorate **TOS'** 55th anniversary, Rebecca Romjin's full character name for Number One was revealed as Una Chin-Riley, with the actor adding: 'Now we finally get to flesh out this character and... she's way more complex than y'all know.' It was also confirmed that Jess Bush would appear as Nurse Christine Chapel and Celia Rose Gooding as Cadet Nyota Uhura.

Romjin added in a live panel discussion that the show features 'Legacy characters with legacy relationships.' This opens up possibilities for relationships between Spock, Uhura and Nurse Chapel, who already have 'legacy relationships' from **TOS**.

We can approach this new show with the confidence that Romjin's Number One is well-defined and has the qualities of a modern woman transported into future fiction and is not burdened with the baggage of a character created and shaped in less enlightened times.

And yet Number One is not so different from the Keeper's assessment of her to Pike in *The Cage*: 'The female you call "Number One" has the superior mind and would produce highly intelligent children. Although she seems to lack emotion, this is largely a pretence. She has often had fantasies involving you.' The 'superior mind' certainly, and the hiding of emotion is still part of her professional façade – hiding her 'freaky' perhaps? And the fantasies about Pike? She blushes when Spock suggests: 'You have made a most careful study of the captain,' so maybe this will be developed. The new Number One would appear to be authentic to her origins, but presented in a more appropriate context.

This an optimistic point to jump off the assessment of sexism and equality in **Star Trek** movies and episodes set on the *Enterprise* in the 2250s and 2260s. It hasn't been a straight, upward trajectory, with a dip from an episode of **TAS** and a significant low point with *Into Darkness*. *Star Trek Beyond*, **Discovery** and **Short Treks**, however, reveal an evolution of the female lead or supporting character, human or otherwise, into nuanced characters. The time of the objectified sex object on **Star Trek** is hopefully firmly in the past.

APPENDIX: ADAPTATIONS

Originally, novelisations were a useful way to revisit movies and TV shows at a time when they were not readily available to rewatch. The range of such tie-ins reduced as home entertainment releases and streaming services enabled viewings of the original content, but they are nevertheless a useful research resource. In all three cases here, the novelisations were not written by the original authors and as such should be regarded as interpretations rather than expressions of the original intent. They are included here to highlight where the novelist has deviated from the original screenplay, either to clarify or emphasise.

Spock's Brain by James Blish, 1972

Between 1967 and 1978, British novelist James Blish adapted the 79 episodes of **Star Trek: TOS** into a series of short stories contained in 13 books (including *Mudd's Angels*).

Spock's Brain is the opening story in November 1972's *Star Trek 8*, published four years after the episode was screened. These adaptations frequently differ from the televised episodes, and on this occasion, based on the material that's included, Blish appears to have used the final draft scripts as his source. Blish also exercises artistic licence when making changes to the stories, so this would have been an opportunity to temper any perceived sexism in the teleplay.

From the very beginning, we're in no doubt how attractive the women are. 'A superbly beautiful woman stood in the precise centre of the bridge... a human woman in all aspects save her extraordinary loveliness... the beautiful intruder.'

The countdown clock is now three days, the lightweight thermal cold weather clothing is back but there's no universal translator. When Luma recovers from Kirk's phaser blast, we read that 'the pretty eyelids opened.' And then after Kirk has been told that Luma has the mind of a child, Blish gives Kirk the line: 'Then she's got a sister who isn't retarded!'

The pain bands are now back on the men's heads, and there are frequent reminders of just how beautiful everyone is: 'The beautiful passenger... the beautiful lady... the women were all physically attractive.' The women's response to the arrival of Kirk and his party is that 'their masculinity caused a stir among the women; but it was the response, not of adult women, but of children on their first visit to the zoo.'

But then the text informs us that 'Something registered in what passed for Kara's brain.' Or 'They *are* retardates, Kirk thought. Getting through to whatever gray matter existed in that beautiful head was going to be tough.' On the matter of Spock's voice saying that his conscience was disturbed by the prospect of betraying such a dependent society, Kirk replies: 'Rubbish!... Pure rationalisation. It's always provoked by a weeping woman.'[187] And because this is based on the final draft script, the ending is the one with the perfume, cuddles and mail propagation. While it's every author's prerogative to make changes as they see fit – here the previously red button that releases the belts is blue, and terrestrial hours are now kyras – it's the addition of the sexist or misogynistic comments that disappoints. This would have been the ideal opportunity to tone

---

[187] Blish, James, *Star Trek 8*, pp9, 21-22, 24, 31.

down the episode's more extreme aspects.[188]

The Lorelei Signal by Alan Dean Foster, 1974

Alan Dean Foster adapted the 22 **TAS** episodes into a series of 10 books between 1974 and 1978.

In his 1974 volume **Star Trek Log 2** he adapted *The Lorelei Signal* into a 57-page story. As with James Blish's adaptation of *Spock's Brain*, this could be an opportunity for the author to tone down any perceived sexism, but while he uses his page count to expand the story, he doesn't pare back the sexist elements. When Uhura asks Chapel to observe the men on the bridge, the nurse coquettishly replies: 'I do that anyway.' The alien women are described as 'giantesses', adding the tired 'Amazonian Women' trope to the story, and there's a moment where Uhura 'wanted to scream, but that would be out of place for an acting commander.' Maybe she's toughened up from the moment where she found out that she might be stranded on the time vortex plane in *The City on the Edge of Forever* and tells Kirk: 'Captain, I'm frightened.'

Foster does however attempt to soften the actions of this androcidal community by showing remorse for their actions; asked why they never sought help from their visitors, they reply that they ae=re 'eternal prisoners of this need which we did not ask for...We have no

---

[188] Blish's biographer shared correspondence from 10 February 1983 where Judith Blish (his wife) revealed that **Star Trek 6-11** (all written under Blish's name except the last where J A Lawrence appears as a collaborator) were actually written by herself and her mother Muriel Lawrence. Quoted in Ketterer, David, *Imprisoned in a Tesseract: The Life and Work of James Blish*, p25.

wish to be murdered as monsters. We have always feared this would happen were we to confess what we have done.' And as a curious coda to the adaptation, a reference is made to the operations carried out on the women at the Federation Fleet Hospital to convert them into regular humanoids: 'Kirk suspected that more than scientific interest motivated the male portion of the staff.'[189]

Star Trek Into Darkness by Alan Dean Foster, 2013

In his novelisation of the scene where Dr Marcus strips down to her underwear in front of Kirk, Foster attempts to justify Kirk's gaze: 'conversations were inevitably more efficacious when conducted face-to-face.' But was he actually looking at her face, since he goes on to reflect that 'regulation Starfleet undergarments, he decided, had rarely looked so fetching.'[190] It's something of a stretch to believe that Marcus' designer underwear is regulation Starfleet attire, but the reader is asked to take his word for it.

---

[189] Foster, Alan Dean, *Star Trek Log 2*, pp81, 91, 113, 118, 126.
[190] Foster, Alan Dean, *Star Trek Into Darkness*, p167.

BIBLIOGRAPHY
Books

Alexander, David, *Star Trek Creator: The Authorised Biography of Gene Roddenberry*. New York, ROC Books, 1994. ISBN 9780451454188.

Asherman, Allan, *The Star Trek Interview Book*. London, Titan Books, 1988. ISBN 9781852861049.

Blair, Karin, *Meaning in Star Trek*. New York, Warner Books, 1977. ISBN 9780446920957.

Block, Paula M and Terry J Erdmann, *Star Trek Costumes*. London, Titan Books, 2015. ISBN 9781783299676.

Collins, Gail, When Everything Changed: *The Amazing Journey of American Women from 1960 to the Present*. New York, Little, Brown and Company, 2009. ISBN 9780316059541

Cowe, Tyler and Alex Tabarrok, *Modern Principles: Macroeconomics*. New York, Worth Publishers, 2011. ISBN 9781429239981.

Cushman, Marc, *These are the Voyages TOS: Season One*. San Diego, Jacobs/Brown Press, 2013. ISBN 9780989283120.

Cushman, Marc, *These are the Voyages TOS: Season Two*. San Diego, Jacobs/Brown Press, 2014. ISBN 9780989238151.

Cushman, Marc, *These are the Voyages TOS: Season Three*. San Diego, Jacobs/Brown Press, 2014. ISBN 9780989238175.

Engel, Joel, *Gene Roddenberry: The Myth and the Man Behind Star Trek*. London, Virgin Books, 1995. ISBN 9780863698798.

Erdmann, Terry J and Paula M Block, *Star Trek 101*. New York, Pocket Books, 2008. ISBN 9780743497237.

Fern, Yvonne, *Gene Roddenberry, The Last Conversation (Portraits of American Genius)*. Berkeley and Los Angeles, University of California Press, 1994. ISBN 9780520088429.

Foster, Alan Dean, *Star Trek Into Darkness*, New York, Gallery Books, 2013. ISBN 9781476716480.

Foster, Alan Dean, *Star Trek: Log Two*. New York, Del Ray, 1974. ISBN 9780345282651.

Gerrold, David, *The World of Star Trek*. New York, Ballantine Books, 1973. ISBN 9780753500903.

Gross, Edward and Mark A. Altman, *The Fifty-Year Mission: The First 25 Years*. New York, Thomas Dunne Books, 2016. ISBN 9871250065841.

Gross, Edward and Mark A. Altman, *The Fifty-Year Mission: The Next 25 Years*. New York, Thomas Dunne Books, 2016. ISBN 9781250089465.

Harris, Jay S, ed. *TV Guide: The First 25* Years. New York, Simon and Schuster, 1978. ISBN 9780671230654.

Friedan, Betty. 'Television and the Feminine Mystique.'

Jones, Nick, ed. *Star Trek: Epic Episodes*. London, Titan Publishing, 2018. ISBN 9781785868795.

Nazarro, Joe 'The Other Gene'.

Ketterer, David, *Imprisoned in a Tesseract: The Life and Work of James Blish*. Kent, State Ohio Press, 1987. ISBN 9780873383346.

Nichols, Nichelle, *Beyond Uhura: Star Trek and Other Memories*. New York, G. P. Putnam's Sons, ISBN 9780752208398.

Palumbo, Donald, ed. *Eros in the Mind's Eye: Sexuality and the Fantastic in Art and Film*. Westport, Greenwood Press, 1986. ISBN 9780313241024.

> Deegan, Mary Jo. 'Sexism in Space: The Freudian Formula in 'Star Trek''.

Reeves-Stevens, Judith and Garfield, *The Art of Star Trek*. New York, Pocket Books, 1995. ISBN 9780671898045.

Roddenberry, Gene, *Star Trek: The Motion Picture – A Novel*. New York, Pocket Books, 1979. ISBN 9780671830885.

Sackett, Susan, *Inside Trek: My Secret Life with Star Trek Creator Gene Rodenberry*. Tulsa, Hawk Publishing, 2013. ISBN 9781930709423.

Sackett, Susan, *Letters to Star Trek*. New York, Ballantine Books, 1977. ISBN 9780345255228.

Sackett, Susan and Gene Roddenberry, *The Making of Star Trek: The Motion Picture*. New York, Pocket Books, 1980. ISBN 9780671791094.

Scheimer, Lou with Andy Mangels, *Lou Scheimer: Creating the Filmation Generation*. Raleigh, TwoMorrows Publishing, 2012. ISBN 9781605490441.

Shatner, William with Chris Kreshki, *Star Trek Memories*. New York, Harper Collins, 1993. ISBN 9780060177348.

Shatner, William with David Fisher, *Up Till Now*. London, Pan Books, 2009. ISBN 9780330452977.

Solow, Herbert F and Robert H Justman, *Inside Star Trek*. New York, Simon & Schuster, 1996. ISBN 9780671896287.

Whitfield, Stephen E. and Gene Roddenberry, *The Making of Star Trek*. New York, Ballantine Books, 1968. ISBN 9780345246912.

Whitney, Grace Lee with Jim Denney, *The Longest Trek: My Tour of the Galaxy*. Fresno, Quill Driver Books, 2007. ISBN 9871884956034.

Periodicals

Playboy. Playboy Enterprises, 1953 – 2020.

> Norden, Eric, 'Playboy Interview: Stanley Kubrick', *Playboy*, Vol. 15, No. 9, September 1968.

> Vadim, Roger, 'Vadim's 'Pretty Maids' – pictorial essay', *Playboy*, Vol. 18, No. 4, April 1971.

> Hochman, David, 'Playboy Interview: J J Abrams'. *Playboy* Vol. 60, No. 4, May 2013.

Starlog. Starlog Group Inc., 1976 – 2009.

> Zsalay, Jeff, 'Gene Roddenberry: The Years Between, The Years Ahead'. *Starlog* #51, October 1981.

> Ellison, Harlan, 'Ellison Reviews TREK'. *Starlog* #33, January 1980.

> Gross, Edward, 'Assignment: "Trek"'. *Starlog* #114, January 1987.

> Gross, Edward, 'Treks into Paradise'. *Starlog* #125, December 1987.

> Jankiewicz, Pat, 'I Stole Spock's Brain'. *Starlog* #319, February

2004.

Film

Colla, Richard A., dir. *The Questor Tapes*. Jeffrey Hayes Productions, Universal Television, 1974.

Daniels, Marc, dir. *Planet Earth*. Warner Bros. Television, 1974.

Donner, Clive, dir. *Spectre*. Norway Productions, 20th Century Fox Productions, 1978.

Fox, Scotty, dir. *Sex Trek II: The Search for Sperm*. Moonlight Entertainment, 1991.

Moxey, John Llewellyn, dir. *Genesis II*. Norway Productions, Warner Bros. Television, 1973.

Romero, George A, dir. *Night of the Living Dead*, Image Ten, 1968.

Vadim, Roger, dir. *Barbarella*. Marianne Productions, Dino de Laurentiis Cinematografica, 1968.

Vadim, Roger, dir. *Pretty Maids All in a Row*. Metro-Goldwyn-Mayer, 1971.

Wise, Robert, dir. *Star Trek: The Motion Picture*, Paramount Pictures, 1979.

Wyler, William, dir. *Funny Girl*. Rastar, 1968.

Television

Bewitched. Screen Gems, Ashmont Productions, 1964-1972.

Samantha's Wedding Present, 1968.

Space Patrol. Mike Moser Productions, 1950-1955.

Star Trek.

> *Star Trek: The Original Series*: Season Three, Paramount Home Entertainment, 2009.
>
> > Disc 6, "To Boldly Go...".

The Wonder Years. ABC, 1988-1993.

> *Just Between Me and You and Kirk and Paul and Carla and Becky*, 1989.

Web

Child, Ben, 'Star Trek Into Darkness Writer Apologises for Underwear Scene', The Guardian, 21 May 2013. https://www.theguardian.com/culture/2013/may/21/star-trek-into-darkness-writer-underwear-scene. Accessed 9 June 2021.

Gilchrist, Todd, 'Star Trek's' Alex Kurtzman Talks Khan, Kirk's Journey and Carol Marcus' Underwear.' CBR.com, 10 September 2013. https://www.cbr.com/star-treks-alex-kurtzman-talks-khan-kirks-journey-carol-marcus-underwear/. Accessed 9 June 2021.

Godfrey, Alex, 'Star Trek Into Darkness: How it was Made, By the People Who Made it'. *The Guardian*, 11 May 2013. https://www.theguardian.com/film/2013/may/11/star-trek-into-darkness-insiders-guide. Accessed 9 June 2021.

Griswold v. Connecticut (1965)
https://www.thirteen.org/wnet/supremecourt/rights/landmark_griswold.html
Accessed 30 September 2021.

Laverty, Lord Christopher, 'Costume Designer Michael Kaplan on

Star Trek Into Darkness'. *Clothes on Film*, 17 May 2013. http://clothesonfilm.com/costume-designer-michael-kaplan-on-star-trek-into-darkness/. Accessed 9 June 2021.

McDowall, Carolyn, 'Mary Quant – Lights, Camera, Action, Mini Skirts Are Back!', *The Culture Concept*, 31 May 2019. https://www.thecultureconcept.com/mary-quant-lights-camera-action-mini-skirts-are-back. Accessed 13 January 2022.

Stratford, Jennifer Juniper, 'Off Hollywood – Denise Crosby'. *Vice*, 2 June 2013. https://www.vice.com/en/article/qbw5yv/off-hollywood-denise-crosby. Accessed 9 June 2021.

'Catching up with TOS Android Andrea'. *StarTrek.com*, 28 July 2019. https://intl.startrek.com/article/exclusive-interview-sherry-jackson-andrea-on-the-original-series. Accessed 9 June 2021.

'Exclusive: J J Abrams Shows a Deleted Star Trek Into Darkness Scene'. *TeamCoco*, unknown date. https://teamcoco.com/video/conan-highlight-showering-cumberbatch. Accessed 9 June 2021.

'Inflation in 1968 and its effect on dollar value'. *In2013dollars.com*. https://www.in2013dollars.com/inflation-rate-in-1968. Accessed 9 June 2021.

'Interview: Bob Blackman – Babes in space?'. *adactio.com*, 7 February 2011 http://bbc.adactio.com/cult/st/interviews/blackman/page14.shtml. Accessed 9 June 2021.

'Interview: Nichelle Nichols - Your Costume'. *adactio.com*, 7 February 2011. http://bbc.adactio.com/cult/st/interviews/nichols/page6.shtml.

Accessed 9 June 2021.

'Licensed and Live: "Spock's Brain" A Retro-Kitsch Hit for the Ages'. *Trekland*, November 2004. http://larrynemecek.com/articles/spocks-brain-live-2005.pdf.

'Original Casting Call' http://stng.36el.com/st-tng/trivia/misc.html. Accessed 9 June 2021.

'Star Trek Into Darkness Official Trailer 2'. *YouTube*, 17 April 2013. https://www.youtube.com/watch?v=RJ1qOs7jkIQ. Accessed 9 June 2021.

'Star Trek Into Darkness – International Trailer – United Kingdom'. *YouTube*, 21 March 2013. https://www.youtube.com/watch?v=jJMYAJ3_0uw. Accessed 9 June 2021.

'Star Trek Into Darkness Spoiler Special: Your Questions Answered'. *MTV News*, 20 May 2013. http://www.mtv.com/news/1707650/star-trek-into-darkness-spoiler-special-burning-questions-answered/. Accessed 9 June 2021.

'Star Trek Sci-Fi Channel Special Edition - Star Trek Insight: Spock's Brain' – 1999'. *YouTube*, 17 January 2021. https://youtu.be/VWuGo29__JA. Accessed 9 June 2021.

'Star Trek: Short Treks' – Contenders TV Nominees Video'. Deadline, 16 August 2020. https://deadline.com/video/star-trek-short-treks-contenders-tv-nominees-video/. Accessed 9 June 2021.

'Trailer Easter Eggs Lead To New Star Trek Into Darkness International Poster Artwork'. TrekMovie.com, 21 March 2013. https://trekmovie.com/2013/03/21/new-star-trek-into-darkness-poster-unveiled-through-hidden-url-in-international-teaser/. Accessed 9 June 2021.

'William Ware Theiss: Awards and Nominations'. Television Academy. https://www.emmys.com/bios/william-ware-theiss. Accessed 9 June 2021.

Audio

Inside Star Trek, 1976, LP, Columbia Records, PC 34279.

ACKNOWLEDGEMENTS

Nick would like to thank:

Paul Simpson, for having the confidence that I could do this, for pushing and encouraging me when needed, and generally keeping the faith.

Andy Smith, for sharing ideas, helping to locate the most obscure articles and being the Spock to my Kirk (or possibly it's the other way round) for so many years.

Marc Cushman, for sharing resources and putting me in touch with Cash Markman – your secret is safe with me!

Justine, for the continuous love, support and belief that I could (and really needed to) do this.

BIOGRAPHY

Nick has been professionally writing about **Star Trek** and TV science fiction since 1995, with his features, reviews and interviews published in print or web versions of *Star Trek Magazine*, *Sci-Fi Bulletin*, *Starburst*, *DreamWatch*, *TV Zone*, *Starlog*, *Cult Times* and *bbc.co.uk*. By his latest count, he has interviewed over 60 cast members and guest stars from the world of **Star Trek**, including Leonard Nimoy, Patrick Stewart, Brent Spiner and all of the main cast of **Voyager**. Nick is also a regular contributor to *Film Score Monthly* and wrote the soundtracks chapter for *The Billboard Encyclopaedia of Music*. He still owns his Mego **Star Trek** action figures from the 1970s, though McCoy's leg is now held in place by Sellotape.

He believes that he has watched *Spock's Brain* more times than any sane human should have to. He can be found on Twitter @NickJJoy.